THE FOLKLORE AND FACTS OF NATURAL NUTRITION

A GUIDE AND REFERENCE BOOK
WITH 100 "MIRACLE" CASE HISTORIES
(IN LETTER FORM), DIET, AND MENUS
SHOWING HOW NUTRITION AND VITAMINS CAN HELP YOU

Fay Lavan and Jean Dalrymple

AN
ARC
BOOK

ARCO PUBLISHING COMPANY, INC.
219 Park Avenue South, New York, N.Y. 10003

An ARC Book
Published 1974 by Arco Publishing Company, Inc.
219 Park Avenue South, New York, N.Y. 10003
by arrangement with Exposition Press

Copyright © 1973 by Fay Lavan and Jean Dalrymple

Library of Congress Catalog Card Number 73-93617

ISBN 0-668-03465-3

Printed in United States of America

Contents

Part One
LETTERS AND CASE HISTORIES OF HEALTH IMPROVEMENT

Part Two

COOKING FOR HEALTH

Part Three

NUTRITIONAL SUPPLEMENTS

Preface

Since my earliest schooldays, I have been interested in food and its preparation. My college major was home economics. At that time, vitamins, minerals in food, amino acids, enzymes were almost unknown. It was not until many years later that I learned that in 1912 the biochemist Dr. Casimir Funk had discovered in food the elements now called vitamins and pointed up their relationship to disease and health.

It was mere chance that brought into my life the important subject of nutrition. I had recurring colds and skin problems. After many years of unsuccessful treatment, a physician specializing in dermatology suggested I might have a vitamin A deficiency, and he prescribed megavitamin doses for me. The results were miraculous and decided me to look further into vitamin therapy.

This was about 1939. Dr. Henry C. Sherman was lecturing at Columbia University on vitamin C and vitamin A, and I attended these lectures. In addition, I wrote for government charts and I purchased every book I could find relating to nutrition. There are now about 150 books in my "health library," as I refer to it, and I have a subscription to every health magazine that I have come across.

My own health had deteriorated after the birth of my two sons, born seventeen months apart. My complaints of extreme fatigue and unexplained feelings of apprehension, plus periodic sinus attacks and myriads of other common ailments, led me from one physician to another. Yet always I was told there was nothing organically wrong with me and that I would "have to learn to live with it."

I then began to apply the knowledge that I had found in such books as the *Agriculture Handbook* # 8 (*Composition of Foods*), published by the U.S. Department of Agriculture.° (This lists some 2483 foods in 100-gr. (3¾ oz.) portions, giving their vitamin, mineral, and calorie content, among other vital information. There are more than those listed that can be used to keep health at its optimal level.) I began to introduce brewers' yeast, high-protein powder, lecithin, and many other foods like them into soups, cereals, meat loaves and many other such recipes. The result was that my husband and I seemed to grow younger as those around us grew older, and we were frequently asked, "Where do you get your vim, vigor, and general physical fitness?"

It was partly to answer these questions that this book was written. It is representative not only of our own experiences but also of those who wrote us and have allowed their letters to be reprinted because they felt as we did. Their letters show that they also were looking for a better way to health, that they also were seeking a way to add happy, healthy, youthful years to their lives. That is why we are presenting their actual experiences—their true case histories. From their letters you will learn of the fantastic improvement that nutrition and vitamins made in the general health of many formerly desperately ill people. The stories could not be more dramatic, and no one can tell these stories better than those who actually lived them and the changes in their lives.

The contributors of the letters are from disparate backgrounds, but they are united by a common link. They have all achieved greatly improved health by using the suggestions, charts, and recipes included in this book.

°For sale by the U.S. Government Printing Office, Washington, D.C. 20402, for $1.50.

Many years of intensive study and research now prove that many things, from anemia to impotence, can be traced to the lack of iron, magnesium, potassium, the B vitamins from B_1 to B_{15}) and the hundreds of other elements missing from our overprocessed foods. This book is meant to make you aware that you must work *with* nature, not *against* her. Doctors, dentists, and others may try to repair you, but depleted tissues mend poorly, if at all, without natural foods, freshly prepared and lightly cooked or raw, as part of your daily regimen.

The menus, foods, and diets we list in Part Two and Part Three are offered not for the treatment or cure of any specific ailment, nor are we promoting any special food products. We urge only that you try an improved program of nutrition gradually so that, as you increase your strength and knowledge, you will enjoy glorious health too.

FAY LAVAN

Foreword

We—Fay and I—have studied nutrition for over twenty years. In the course of those years, we have tried to pass on our personal findings to friends and acquaintances who were interested in, or sometimes just curious about, our theories and experiences with organic foods, food supplements, vitamins, and minerals.

Actually, it was only through Fay Lavan's influence that I began an intensive reading and serious study of health books, magazines and articles. I was enormously impressed by Fay's radiant beauty and boundless energy, and our very first luncheon together was devoted to a lengthy discussion of the foods and vitamins Fay said were responsible for her well-being.

Today, as the mother of two sons, aged thirty-three and thirty-one, and the grandmother of three boys and one girl, Fay Lavan has the same slim, youthful figure, the same glowing complexion, the same famous vitality that were so evident at that first luncheon some twenty years ago.

Just as impressive is the appearance of her husband, Peter I. B. Lavan. He looks, lives, plays golf, and dances like an energetic man well under fifty, despite the fact that he has carried on an active law practice for *over* fifty years, during which he has filled in his "spare time" with presidential and governmental appointments! He walks vigorously ten miles a day, at a pace exceeding the U.S. Army's official rate, and he weighs today what he weighed as a senior at college. Like Fay, he seems a perfect example of what can be accomplished by following the simple rules for healthful living suggested by Fay Lavan thirty-seven years ago.

Long before the publication of Dr. Linus Pauling's controversial book, *Vitamin C, and the Common Cold,* Fay was proposing to her many friends and acquaintances the use of this vitamin as a protection against the common cold, and they often expressed astonishment to find that it worked. Also, she early on suggested using vitamin E (the oil from a capsule) on minor burns (it now is used in many hospitals for third-degree burns), as well as for skin blemishes, small cuts, canker sores, and shingles, in addition, of course, to advocating that it be taken internally for general well-being. And, always, she emphasized proper nutrition.

As a youngster, I grew up in a health-conscious family where meals included such unusual items—that is, thought at that time to be unusual—as yogurt, "raw" milk, and unsulfured molasses, and where we avoided all fried foods, white bread, white sugar, coffee, and tea. However, it became inexpedient to follow this regimen, through years of working and traveling, and most of these proper eating habits were forgotten. They were remembered once more only when the conductor Leopold Stokowski brought up the subject of good nutrition when he offered at luncheon a salad he had made of grated raw carrots, celery, apples, nuts, and raisins. His menu also included cottage cheese with yogurt, and herb tea prepared with mint fresh from his garden. Much of the luncheon hour was spent discussing his firm belief in "health discipline," as he termed it, which he has followed to this day. At the age of eighty-six, he is still going strong as the vigorous conductor and music director of the famous American Symphony Orchestra.

George Bernard Shaw, at another delicious vegetarian luncheon, during which he labeled all meat-eaters "cannibals" for partaking of "the dead bodies of our brother-animals," also lectured me on my eating and drinking habits. After that lunch, more than a week passed before I could tackle a lamb chop at the dinner table. Shaw himself never ceased to function. He was busy writing an article for the London *Times* when he died at ninety-four.

Gloria Swanson, past seventy, still slim and beautiful, who recently starred on Broadway in *Butterflies Are Free*, is another "health nut," as she likes to call herself, who shared her nutritional and beauty secrets with me. But it was only after my initial meeting with Fay Lavan that any of this good advice took hold and was, little by little, put to use.

Both Fay and I have had many experiences with persons who say they were helped by our suggestions and who thanked us for them, often by letter. As the years went by, we had (since both of us are "savers") a large accumulation of interesting material from our "case histories" running the gamut of ailments and all insisting they had been helped—even cured—by natural methods.

One day, almost simultaneously, we arrived at the thought that it might be a good idea to compile a book from letters so others could benefit from the stories told in these personal histories. In addition, we decided to expand the book to include other pertinent matter: vitamin charts, menus, recipes, personal suggestions, and the like. Fay decided to do the necessary research, which took two years and the study of more than 150 books.

It is our belief that this collection of letters and suggestions makes interesting reading even if you are a skeptic. Possibly, the information it contains could guide you to improved health and happiness. We do not say that vitamin therapy can cure pneumonia, or whooping cough, or measles, or even the flu (vitamin C wards off colds but not influenza). But we do believe that this book, by acquainting you with individual cases of those who benefited from changes in dietary habits and the use of food supplements, may encourage you to emulate them.

There will be many readers who will disagree with some (or even all!) of these letters, but read them with an open mind. Included is a letter from a woman who was scheduled for an operation to relieve continual numbness in her right leg. We suggested that she try changing her usual inadequate diet (we thought), and also take vitamin B_6 (pyridoxine). She never had the operation, soon recovered the full use of her leg, and returned to her favorite diversion: dancing.

Then there is a letter from a man of sixty who bemoaned the fact that, although in his younger years he had been an outstanding athlete, as he grew older it became more and more difficult for him even to walk because of severe pain in his knees. Again B_6 and proper nutrition helped. He now plays golf almost every day and wouldn't think of using a cart!

All the letters which follow are authentic. Some have been shortened and others edited, although in most cases the writers have been left to express in their own words and thoughts the benefits they have reaped through a knowledge of better nutrition, food supplements, and vitamins. They are not presented here as a panacea—but a reading of them can't hurt you and could help you.

JEAN DALRYMPLE

Introduction: How to Be Perpetually Young

Old age is only one among the many woes of the world, and its course is no longer irrevocable. There is a cure, and a hope for a reversal of it. Our personal experiences and observations confirm our belief that food is the best of all medicines.

It should not be our destiny to become ill, feeble, and senile. The science of geriatrics has proved that the use of fresh wholesome foods containing all vitamins and minerals can help you and your family remain in good health at any age. We have had many letters from persons in their eighties and even nineties who are reaping the benefits of proper nutrition.

The facts we give you about food values are your potential for eternal youth. You will find this new way of life intriguing. In Part Three of this book you will find charted for you the additions to your diet that you need. And you can learn to enrich your own and new recipes in Part Two.

"How to Be Perpetually Young" really understates the theme, for indeed, the first aim should be for general good health. The other benefits that will of themselves follow are feelings of serenity, relaxation, and contentment—a sound mind in a sound body.

If you have been feeling that all the wrong things have been happening to you lately, or that life has been cheating you or passing you by, you may find, as we did, that the secret can be laid to your food habits. If you want to do something to change this, there is a way out—a way that can be as rewarding and interesting as you want to make it, one that will bring you the most enjoyable and personally satisfying living.

The Folklore and Facts of Natural Nutrition represents a distinct departure from orthodox treatment in texts on vitamins, minerals, organic foods, and the entire subject of nutrition since it is largely a presentation of personal experiences from people who were seeking simple answers to their health problems and found their answers, as we did, through nutrition.

Hundreds of books have been written on nutrition, and we have most of them in our combined libraries. Then why add another? you may ask. As we combed through our books and periodicals, we found that, despite prodigious research, we were left in a quandary, as are many other persons, about vitamin supplements. We all want to know is there such a thing as an excess of vitamins. How much can a person take without overdoing it? Is is possible to take too much of anything, including foods and vitamins? We will try to give you the answers here. For here are detailed the experiences of more than one hundred persons who have benefited from changes in their diets, ranging from simply giving up sweet snacks full of calories, TV dinners with no nutrition, or even just turning away from canned foods, to switching to good wholesome food and a program of vitamins and mineral supplements.

There are two reasons for taking vitamins: (1) to prevent vitamin deficiency and (2) as a therapeutic measure, when a vitamin deficiency has been diagnosed through blood chemistry and urinalysis. Your physician can arrange for you to be tested for many vitamin and mineral deficiencies, and he can make proper recommendation for the vitamin dosage you need. Or you can buy one of the self-help testing kits available for testing the vitamin C level in the urine. This vitamin must be replaced daily and kept at the maximum level to prevent colds and back problems. Recommended doses for this vitamin are printed on the bottle. As you take extra amounts (you may want to take more as more information becomes available and benefits from increased amounts become known), the increase in units or milligrams should be gradual, or you may develop symptoms of overdosage: headaches, diarrhea, or flushing. There have been cases of vitamin poisoning reported in adults and children; however, these have been mainly for situations where a very young child had swallowed the entire contents of a bottle of vitamins or where very large doses were taken by an adult or given to a child over a long period of time, either by mistake, or through the misconception that if "a little helps, a greater amount will remedy the ailment faster."

Folk medicine reaches far back in time. Since remotest antiquity, men have depended on folk medicine for many cures. While they are not the products of scientific research, the practice of using them to cure many ailments has been handed down from generation to generation, even to today. For instance, Dr. D. C. Jarvis in his book *Folk Medicine: A Vermont Doctor's Guide to Good Health* (published by Holt, Rinehart and Winston) tells of the many medically acceptable uses of honey and apple-cider vinegar formerly considered folklore.

A number of other physicians have realized the importance of folk medicine and written about it. Dr. Sam Roberts of the University of Kansas Medical School in his book *Ear, Nose and Throat Dysfunctions* (published by C. C. Thomas) suggests the use of cider vinegar and sea salt as a more efficacious remedy for ear, nose, and throat ailments than medications used by organized medicine. He also stressed the importance of an improved diet, with particular emphasis on brewers' yeast as the main source of B vitamins, and insisted that his patients follow such a diet for at least thirty days before spending time on extensive tests. Dr. Roberts has also written a book, *Exhaustion: Causes and Treatment* (Rodale), in which he fully covers the subject of fatigue and sugar metabolism.

Dr. John M. Ellis of the Titus County Memorial Hospital in Mount Pleasant, Texas, in his book *The Doctor Who Looked at Hands* (Arc Books), explains his work with pyridoxine (vitamin B_6) which provided clinical proof that a vitamin B_6 deficiency often does exist in man, and that it will, when replaced, "move fluids in the body; limber arthritic joints; and cause patients to overcome edema [swelling] of pregnancy." (The pecan is particularly rich in this vitamin.)

Dr. Roger Williams of Texas University has stated: "The whole nutritional chain of life is needed by cells with a deficient environment." Dr. Rogers was the discoverer of pantothenic acid.

Dr. Linus Pauling's work with vitamin C is well known and has had a profound effect on the treatment of the common cold. Although widely acclaimed as an authentic cure, vitamin C must be used correctly to abort a cold; how to use it is explained in the section on colds (in Part One).

The body needs not just one but *all* vitamins and minerals for health. If you want to continue to be young, in body and spirit, you must follow the precept of eating correctly.

As your knowledge about foods and vitamins deepens and as your vitality increases, you will better understand the relationship between emotions and illness and how to cope with fatigue and lack of sexual interest.

While there does exist extensive literature on nutrition and child development, it is not generally aimed at the lay person. Basic nutritional principles should be taught in the schools, at all levels, to combat the effects of nutritional deprivation. The inadequate luncheon meals generally served at schools are slowly becoming a public issue. The mother must be taught how important it is to learn about food values and how to get full nutrition for her family from every food dollar. Part Three contains extensive information on vitamins, minerals, and food supplements. We hope you will refer to it often!

Part One

LETTERS AND CASE HISTORIES OF HEALTH IMPROVEMENT

"Many receive advice; only the wise profit by it."

—CYRUS

"Bad men live that they may eat and drink, whereas good men eat and drink that they may live."

—SOCRATES

"Tell me what you eat and I will tell you what you are."

—ABS, 1755-1826

In these days of indigestion
It is oftentimes a question
As to what to eat and what to leave alone,
For each microbe and bacillus
Has a different way to kill us
And in time they always claim us for their own."

—RAY ATWELL, 1880

On Allergies

My husband was a sales manager for many years, and to him befell the duty of entertaining customers and out-of-town dignitaries. At fifty, he was an alcoholic, and he smoked six packs of cigarettes a day.

At the age of fifty-five, he suddenly realized that these habits were responsible for his rapidly declining health. He then started to devote himself to regaining some of the accustomed vigor and good health he had enjoyed in his twenties. We worked together to change his eating habits, and this included adding B vitamins and all other vitamin supplements to his diet.

However, when he was sixty-five, he suddenly developed the classic symptoms of adrenal insufficiency. He was allergic to everything, but to beef least of all, and the doctor suggested an all-steak-and-hamburger diet, as he believed that beef contained all the vitamins my husband would need, when taken with adrenal-cortex extract injections.

We are not certain whether it was a result of this restricted diet, but his eyes were developing cataracts. Alarmed by this new turn of events, he resumed taking all the vitamins and broadened his diet to include organ meats. Within six months time he was able to watch television, he was able to drive once again, and he feels that his sight is improving daily. At his last examination, his eye doctor (an antivitamin man) was astonished at his continued improvement.

There is not much doubt in our minds that the twenty years of hard drinking and smoking were responsible for the adrenal trouble, and we are now very happy that all the problems are under control, due to the improvement in diet and the vitamin supplements.

For years I have had an imbalance in my glandular system, and until I began treating it nutritionally, I had numerous food allergies. For three months I have been taking organic vitamins and I am now about back to normal and can eat everything but eggs.

My husband is following the same diet except that he does not eat meat. Our physician, who is interested in nutrition, has prescribed red marrow-bone pills, which he says have the same food value as meat. Now my husband, too, I am happy to say, is enjoying improved health.

On Anemia

When I left my home in Europe several years ago, I was fortunate in finding a position with a family that used only organic vegetables and fruits and supplemented their diets with vitamins and minerals. I could not understand why they never used white sugar but only honey and molasses, why they ate only brown rice, and why everything they ate was enriched with high-protein powder or skim-milk powder. There was always wheat germ on the table as well as lecithin and brewers' yeast.

It took me some time to learn this new way of life. At first I did not want to try so many new things, but gradually, little by little, I started to follow the new ways of eating. Why did I do this? These people were old enough to be my parents and yet were vigorous and full of good humor and wonderful to be with.

I had developed a hacking cough from cigarettes and was always tired from lack of sleep because I coughed so much at night. Now I was determined to change. I started with a vitamin that had everything in it from A to Z. I learned to eat vegetables and fruits, and did everything my employers did. Then I returned to my home for a six-week visit. During those six weeks, I taught my dearest friend, who had been ill with anemia for several years, everything I knew. She gave up her black coffee and bun for breakfast and took in their place a cup of camomile tea, one egg, and one slice of whole-grain bread. With this meal she took her vitamins and desiccated-liver powder and brewers' yeast. She took vitamins B_{12} and C three times daily, and vitamin E in the morning. For lunch she had liver and salad, and each day had at least 60 grams of protein. After six weeks I accompanied her to her physician, who was surprised to find that for the first time in several years her blood count was normal. He suggested she continue this program and said that he was going to try it on his other patients.

I was happy that I could help her and myself.

On Arteriosclerosis

When I realized I did not want to be a statistic and learned that I was one of the nearly one million adults with arteriosclerosis, I began my search for an answer to my problem. My father had suffered a stroke at about my age.

The drugs and advice I had been offered for nearly one year did not seem to help my shortness of breath, pain around the heart, lack of sex interest, low morale, and fatigue.

I read that the National Health Education Committee had just released a study of the advances made by medical science and that, in defiance of these great advances, heart attacks, strokes, mental illness and cancer were still the major killers and cripplers, despite the money being spent on research in them.

What concerned me most was the diagnosis I had received of arteriosclerosis, sometimes called hardening of the arteries. It is the condition that underlies heart attacks and strokes and is the leading cause of death in the United States. In arteriosclerosis, there is a thickening of the walls of the arteries caused by fatty deposits. Now I wanted to know how to rid myself of these fatty deposits. By chance I came across a health magazine at the home of a friend who was interested in nutrition. I learned that research had been going on in this since 1942. I knew I could not change my eating habits all at once, but would try to do it gradually. I read that 3 tablespoons of lecithin granules, a soybean derivative, taken daily with or as a breakfast cereal, or 2 tablespoons taken with each meal, had helped others bring down their cholesterol count in from three to six months, and I decided to start on the same program. Later I learned about other vitamins and supplements that should be taken with lecithin, and so added vitamin E, vitamin B$_6$, and magnesium in the form of dolomite, all considered important by many researchers and biochemists, to my intake. As my knowledge grew, my confidence and health were restored.

On Arthritis

Dr. Melvin Page has written a fine book about diet as a weapon against arthritis: Degeneration—Regeneration. *Dr. Page feels the source of arthritic problems lies in an imbalance in the calcium-phosphorus ratio of the blood. It has also been said that most arthritic victims consume large amounts of carbohydrates. In checking their food habits, it has been found that they consume many cups of coffee a day, each sweetened with sugar, and invariably, candy, cookies, cake, and canned sweet fruits are part of their daily diet.*

Mental and emotional stress, poor sleeping positions, and poor general posture have also been blamed for arthritic symptoms.

Dr. deCoti-Marsh of England and many other researchers agree that the initial approach to the treatment of many types of arthritis is a diet which will correct the lowered efficiency of body chemistry. A full nutritional program should include alfalfa tea, plenty of pure water, blackstrap molasses, and vitamin and mineral supplements.

I had visited many doctors' offices (for arthritis of my fingers), always chilled by the professional cheerless verdict: "There is no cure for this condition. Take aspirin to check the pain"—as many as ten a day were suggested—"and if it doesn't help, come back and we will try cortisone injections."

I wondered how I could have been overtaken by this physical catastrophe. I needed to be well to earn a living as a secretary. Desperately, I tried all the so-called fringe medicine in hopes of a cure, but all the treatments convinced me of the futility of the procedures I had been following.

I continued to search, this time via the less costly route of the printed page. Thus, I came on a nutrition writer in whose popular book I found the answer which led to the course that changed my life.

I learned that arthritis and rheumatism are caused basically by too much food as well as by unsuitable foods. The kind and amount of food one eats determines what kinds and amounts of poisons are built up in the body. If the elimination of these is hindered in any way, then the symp-

toms which we call arthritis or rheumatism are triggered.
From this book I learned about nutrition. I learned that
starches and sweets would have to be eliminated from my
diet or kept to a minimum, and that my system had to be
cleaned out and kept clean through elimination. Fresh fruits,
salads, lightly steamed vegetables, avocado, and nuts were
suggested as a start to new eating habits. It seemed impossible for me to give up the old way of eating—processed
foods, canned foods, sugar, white bread, coffee and a Danish
for the coffee break—but I persevered. My health improved,
my fingers improved, and I am happy to say I am back at
my job full time.

I doubt that we, husband and wife, both seventy-three,
would be alive today had I not discoverd health magazines.
They inspired us to leave the city. We hunted and found
some trees and a small cottage on an acre in lovely moun-
tainous country where we could grow our own food.

This year, our third, we picked tomatoes 15½ inches in
circumference. Potatoes—a few—were 1 pound 5 ounces
each. (I weighed them.) We had asparagus, Swiss chard,
huge leeks, comfrey (which we use, fresh, for tea, and dried
for winter—cheap vitamin C). Fifteen vegetables in all, and
ducks, some in my freezer.

I use no coffee or tea. Alfalfa tea with honey—no sugar.
To me, it's poison. Honey for all sweetening. No soft drinks.
No popular frying preparations. I use soy oil where necessary
for frying.

I use spring water with a little country-made cider, since
reading about pure water in a health magazine. I take no end
of vitamins—A, E, C (from rose hips)—and bone meal, etc.
Without them, I would not have recovered so quickly from
an operation.

My arthritis is nearly gone, both because of my diet and

because I use my hands even when they hurt. I play the organ daily for exercise—no aspirin for me. But I have learned to squeeze, not twist, anything when washing by hand. Twisting seems to be hard on finger joints.

In May 1971 I developed severe pains in my back, my left arm, then my left leg. I went to a health club for exercise, hot baths, steam room, but it was not much help.

I went to a doctor, one of the best and most expensive, and had an X ray which showed arthritis. He prescribed pills, but there was no relief. I took aspirin and it offered little help.

One day I tried molasses (blackstrap) which helped immediately. I am now using it three times weekly, and after three weeks I have had no pain of any kind and am following a full-nutrition program.

My knees were going progressively bad with arthritis, to the point where I had to stop dancing and bowling. Three days ago I made up a batch of alfalfa tea as I had learned it was helpful, except I went a step further: instead of throwing the seed away after straining the tea, I added a little honey to the seed. It made a very good breakfast food.

I have been drinking a quart a day of strong alfalfa tea for three days and now I can bend my knees enough to tie my shoelaces. Another two weeks and I will be able to resume dancing and bowling.

On Asthma

For over twenty years I have been considered a "health crank" by some people, and admired as an example of "practicing what she preaches" by others. I started preparing for pregnancy three years before this happy event took place, building my own body to be a storehouse of resources for the child I planned to conceive.

In due course, my lovely baby was born, nursed, and weaned to as nearly a natural diet as urban life affords (never a can of baby food in my house), and his growth and development were a joy. Yet at the age of four and a half, he suddenly was struck with a serious attack of asthma, for no apparent reason, and it lasted for a week.

For two years after this, chronic attacks of asthma followed. We never knew when they would strike or how long they would last. Constant pediatric attention provided only temporary symptomatic relief with medication and vaporizers, and I believe it was only prayer that saved his life.

We saw allergists, psychologists, specialists of every kind. We were advised to get rid of the dog, to have no wool around the house, to avoid feather pillows. All along I was observing the best of nutritional principles (I made my own bread, used wheat germ in everything, raw foods and such, along with well-selected supplements), but the pattern of acute chronic asthma remained unchanged.

Something from my reading in health books came to my mind: that vitamin E increases the body's ability to utilize oxygen. Perhaps my son, although well supplied by ordinary standards, had an individual need for more? I figured there could be no harm in giving him 100 milligrams daily of alpha-tocopherol, and I started him on this at age six and a half as he was convalescing from pneumonia.

As of that day, eleven years ago, the attacks came to an end. We have had no more asthma, and no more pneumonia, even though we live in one of the most smog-congested areas in the country. Even though I have little control over the diet that a seventeen-and-a-half-year-old-boy consumes when he is at school or away from home, he has rarely missed his supplements, which include (now) 200 units of vitamin E daily.

I'm not saying vitamin E cures asthma. I'm saying that my son, who was in a fair way to become crippled with this disease over a period of two years, has had no further lung involvement since the regular employment of alpha-tocopherol in his daily diet.

On the Bladder

During a recent medical checkup, I was informed that urine tests showed I had a slightly abnormal bacteria count. The nurse telephoned to say that the doctor thought it advisable for me to take an antibiotic for five days. This came as a surprise to me, as I felt well and had been following a full nutritional program for many years. My only complaint was frequent visits to the bathroom at night, and no one could give me an answer to this problem, so I accepted it as part of the aging process.

When I inquired whether there was some natural method of handling this problem (as I am allergic to drugs), she insisted this was a mild drug, and it was to be taken for just five days. I asked the pharmacist for only one day's supply —only four pills—and said if I was not allergic to them I would fill the balance of the prescription. (Many pharmacists will not do this as they find it a nusiance to make up the label and entry, but they do have a minimum quantity they will fill and even this saves money.)

After taking just one tablet, my eye was swollen, red,

and itchy four hours later. I called the doctor and he suggested taking cortisone to clear the allergy, but this I refused to take.

A friend suggested a doctor interested in treating the patient from the nutritional point of view. For the frequent urinary problem he suggested eliminating parsley, celery, asparagus, and milk, and limiting all drinking after dinner. For the infection he suggested a liquid diet for twenty-four to forty-eight hours of apple juice or water, but apple juice is pleasanter and more nourishing. The liquid diet proved helpful and harmless.

He also suggested that anyone with kidney or bladder trouble keep the feet warm at night by brisk rubbing with a soft natural bristle brush, and said it is also important to be careful of drafts from air conditioning and any kind of dampness. I am happy to report that I am now sleeping five hours or more without a disturbance and am grateful that there are still practitioners who are interested in natural methods.

I had many visits to doctors for a water-retention problem. All diuretics disagreed with me. I was also allergic to the one I purchased at the health-food store.

In a health magazine I read that a physician using natural methods of treatment suggested a diet of cucumber juice, from one glass to as much as a quart for a period of forty-eight to seventy-two hours. A watermelon diet has also been suggested but it could only be followed when watermelon is in season and easily available.

I used the cucumber-juice diet and later added the juice of parsley, celery and asparagus, as these are also diuretic vegetables. It is also important to learn which vegetables contain high amounts of sodium, as these add to water retention and edema. One pint of water weighs one pound of weight, and an excess lost by removal with diuretics causes a lot of potassium which must be replaced.

I learned that vitamin C and B$_6$ are helpful. I learned to increase my protein, gradually upped my brewers' yeast to 3 tablespoons, and kept my carbohydrates to a minimum. I added 2 tablespoons of vegetable oil to get essential fatty acids.

My balloonlike figure gradually decreased, as if the air were let out of a balloon. As my figure improved, so did my energy and my morale.

On Bone Healing

Bone meal as a form of calcium aids in cases of slow healing, premature aging, leg cramps, and excessive tooth decay.

Dr. Henry C. Sherman in his laboratory experiments shows that amounts of calcium far above the generally accepted minimum not only do no harm but actually make for a longer and healthier life.

Bone meal and dolomite contain magnesium, which is a neglected mineral. It is helpful in healing bone fractures of various types and will improve both nails and hair as well as help equilibrium.

I would like to relate an experience I had a few years ago. A very dear friend of mine broke her femur in an auto accident. She lay in the hospital for two months, without healing. The doctors, after surgery, were still baffled.

Upon visiting her in the hospital I convinced her to try bone-meal tablets. After a month on eight tablets of bone meal per day, the X ray showed a definite healing of the bone. Then the doctor's advice was to double the dose.

She was in her fifties when this happened, but is now in good shape. I also convinced her of the necessity of vitamins for health.

One warm day in August, as I was walking my pet dog, I turned my ankle in the damp grass and heard the sound of a cracking bone. I crawled to my neighbor's house, and we went directly to the hospital, where we saw the doctor. The X ray showed three breaks. Eventually, two of the breaks healed, and the doctor said that in my case, surgery might be necessary to seal the remaining break. My husband went directly to the health store and bought some bone meal and vitamin E capsules, which I took faithfully. After four weeks, we went back to the doctor for X rays, and the doctor had to admit I had made a miraculous recovery.

I was in a bad auto accident two years ago. My chest was injured, but no bones were broken, which I know was due to my taking bone meal every day for some years. The diagnostic tests showed my heart was damaged. The doctors were giving me digitalis and other medicine, which only made me feel worse.

I threw their medicine away and upped my vitamin E intake from 100 to 400 IU daily. I also raised my vitamin C intake to 500 IU,* and in a month I was breathing normally again. Last year I had my gallstones removed, and on the third day was walking in the corridor with no trouble or pain. My doctor was amazed that at my age (will be seventy-two at Christmas) I did so well.

I know it was following my nutrition program that did it. I am still working part time as a security guard, besides raising most of the vegetables I eat in my own backyard and do-

*International units.

ing my own cooking. The best move I ever made was to read about nutrition and follow it.

Being a reader of health magazines for many years, I have tried to follow most of their suggestions for better health. One of these, of course, advocates the use of bone meal daily. I have been taking this now for several years. Reading of others' experiences in falling and not getting any broken bones has caused me to write this letter telling you of my own fall just two months ago.

I was on a ladder set on top of a porch, trying to repair a small defect in the gable of a two-story house, when the ladder slipped on the tin roof of the porch and the ladder, myself, and everything fell directly to the ground, about sixteen feet. I fell on my back, full weight, and the edge of a ditch along the porch caught the small of my back, and turned it backward like a jackknife. I had my hip pocket full of tools, pliers, tin-snip, etc., and these tools punched into my side, hitting the top of my hipbone and the lower part of my short ribs. I was hauled to the hospital, and the X rays showed no broken bones, which astonished the doctors as well as me and my friends, very much.

I am seventy-eight years of age. Many of my acquaintances of this same age have suffered small falls resulting in broken hips. But the doctors who have made several close examinations of me since the fall still insist that there were no broken bones. Naturally, I give all the credit to the fact that I have taken these bone-meal pills for so long.

Incidentally, I have a brother two years my junior who fell from the bottom step of a small step ladder, twelve to eighteen inches from the ground, and he broke two bones in one arm, damaged the bones of one hand, and fractured several ribs in the fall. He has never taken bone meal and seems uninterested in the health-food regimen that I have been following for more than a score of years.

I thought perhaps this case may be of interest to you, as I firmly believe that the bone-meal theory so long advocated surely has much merit in practice.

Eight years ago my family (three children) started taking bone meal after reading an article in one of the health magazines. This year our dental bills were $15. I can remember when they were $150 to $175 per year. Who is responsible for keeping this information from the public?

What about the articles that appeared only in health magazines warning of the dangers of cyclamates six years ago? Does there have to be a major catastrophe before the public is alerted?

Anyone recommending eating natural foods instead of processed, or using natural organic fertilizer for gardening (to get the most vitamins and minerals from natural produce) was labeled a "food nut" or a "crackpot." Those of us that continued to "watch the pot" can be thankful for all the advice we were given and we followed. Articles about B vitamins for nerves—we were told: Who needs B vitamins for nerves? But B vitamins have no side effects, no toxic reaction. The manufactureres of tranquilizers, of course, would keep us ignorant of its benefits.

About the controversial vitamin E: a relative of mine has taken vitamin E for a number of years. Last time she had an examination, her doctor was quite puzzled because she had what he called a marked improvement in her heart condition. It was the reverse of what generally happens with age.

If you look around you you can see the gullibility of the people who refuse to recognize what the forces around them are creating. How long can the public be deceived?

*   *   *

It is eighteen years now that the knowledge of nutrition I gained from health magazines has helped my family in many ways. When I started, I was discouraged over my poor health, having been to many doctors without receiving help, only more complications. All was solved when I changed my diet and started taking vitamins. I was feeling younger every year (I am now sixty) until my water-skiing accident two years ago in June, when I broke my right leg near the hip. Now I am walking and feeling fine, back to my normal self, and have only a slight limp, all because, I feel, all these years I was taking vitamins.

My sixteen-year-old son's accident was so serious the doctors did not expect him to live. He was in the hospital for four months. All this time, before, during, and after, he was given from seven to ten vitamins—brewers' yeast, vitamins C, E, A, and D, bone meal, dolomite, natural iron, and for the last few months, kelp, niacin for circulation, and rutin to combat radioactive substances from X rays.

The doctors did what they could, but I doubt that he would have been normal again without the precious vitamins and proper diet, and consequent good health. I feel sure the vitamins saved my son's life. His doctors are still flabbergasted at his amazing recovery.

Following a full nutritional program is indispensable to good health and better living.

On Circulation

I had trouble with my legs. I had a burning sensation whether on or off my feet. They were painful, and I was getting varicose veins. For years I have had no processed foods and was taking what I considered adequate vitamin supplements.

After reading about vitamins B₆ and B₃ (niacin) I added these gradually, and also vitamin E, to my program. Hydrocloric acid in the form of apple-cider vinegar—1 teaspoon to a glass of water with a little honey—or in tablet form had also been suggested. These help to assimilate the food and vitamins. Many people do not produce enough hydrocloric acid as they get older.

With all these added to my regular routine, I am happy to say my feet and legs are now functioning normally.

On Colds

The avoidance of colds is important. There are as many ways of treating a cold as there are patent medicines on the market, and everyone has his favorite remedy. There are those who say, "Feed a cold"; others say, "Starve a fever," which often accompanies a cold. Many people are able to abort a cold by large doses of vitamin C, as suggested by Dr. Linus Pauling. There is, by the way, a difference in the benefits one receives from natural C—from rose hips or acerola—as opposed to the ascorbic acid in tablet form. There even have been complaints of discomfort from the use of the latter type of ascorbic acid in large doses.

The fifty-odd nutrients needed by humans affect one another's requirements. There have been studies on the interaction of vitamins C and B₆ (pyridoxine) and protein. In these, when the subjects were placed on a diet deficient in B₆, the levels of vitamin C dropped, and when B₆ was added to the diet, the vitamin C in the blood rose. The B₆ require-

ments were correlated with protein intake, and the greater the protein, the greater the need for vitamin B_6 to help metabolize the protein.

Many people have found vitamin A as well as C helpful in preventing colds.

Being a delicate child with a small frame, I was host to all ills, but particularly upper-respiratory infections—I had pneunomia six times and should have been dead long ago. So I early became interested in anything which would keep me healthy and give me pep. For years I have taken great quantities of all vitamins.

But I work like a coolie and I never get enough sleep. I read everything I can find on nutrition and health and practice it as best I can. Thank heavens, I learned the yoga stomach-lift years ago. It saved my appendix and keeps me feeling fit. Exercise is important to feel great.

Oh yes, with vitamin C, I not only don't have pnuemonia and influenza but I seldom have a cold.

My family has been taking garlic caspules for the past two years, and we have gone unscathed through two bad flu epidemics. The children were in school last year when half their classmates were out with flu. I was in and out of homes taking care of flu victims and never once had so much as a sign of flu symptoms.

I am giving a talk on health at my church next Sunday, the day I will be eighty years old. And I will tell them truthfully that I have not had a cold in seventy years.

When I was ten, a fine old doctor of eighty-five gave a health talk at our church. He said he'd tell us the most important thing he'd learned fifty years of practice on how to prevent colds.

When we are ripe for a cold, we are overloaded with waste products and should not add more fuel—food. So, at the very first sign of a cold, miss a meal or two, then eat lightly of fruits or vegetables for another meal or two—and you have it whipped. If you eat a heavy meal too soon, you are sunk. The cold gets hold of you and you will have the standard miserable week or ten days getting rid of it. You must abort it at the start. People are afraid to fast. But it will not hurt them.

It seems a shame for the old doctor's discovery made in fifty years of practice to go to waste. If there is any way to keep the good doctor's discovery going, that's great. I added massive doses of vitamin C to the old doctor's regimen—twenty years ago.

Last fall a friend was having difficulty throwing off a case of the flu. He had read Dr. [Linus] Pauling and was taking ascorbic acid, 1,200 milligrams per day. He complained to me of discomfort in the stomach.

I suggested to him the rose-hips type of vitamin C and he upped the intake to 1,800 milligrams per day, with no discomfort, and he was soon feeling well again.

My first experience with vitamin supplements came when I had a series of prolonged colds lasting almost two years. After about eighteen months of unsuccessful treatments of various kinds, my doctor, almost as a last resort, prescribed a therapeutic vitamin formula with a daily intake of 50,000 units of vitamin A.

I promptly got well, and have remained well so far as colds and flu are concerned as long as I continue to take not less than 12,500 units of vitamin A.

This, of course, was an improvement. I started a full nutritional program and a major improvement took place in the last two or three years.

This past winter, I tried something new on myself—a quickie, too. It works fast. When I feel a cold starting and get the sneezes and a runny nose, I boil about 2 cups of water in a small open pot and dash in some garlic salt—about ¼ teaspoon. When it reaches a boil, I take the pot off the stove and let the steam gently waft up into my nostrils, sniffing it but not inhaling deeply. The discharge stops and I'm able to go about my work. Somehow the cold doesn't get a hold on me, I'm happy to say!

When I went to school, colds and flu were my constant companions all through the winter months. And I was weak for I could not get much sleep because of coughing. Every time I took cold, I lost my appetite and felt completely miserable. Cough medicine helped some but did not keep a new cold back.

My family and I had never heard of vitamins. We did not know they existed. Then one day I brought a science book home. I was in high school by this time. My dad always liked to read my schoolbooks. He picked up the book and began turning the pages. A special page caught his eye. It was about vitamin A and how it fights the common cold. "Look, here is something for you," Dad said excitedly. "It's worth a try."

Dad bought a bottle of cod liver oil for me and I took it according to directions. In about a week or ten days my cold disappeared and I felt so much better.

I continued using vitamin A and there were quite a few winters when I didn't even have the slightest cold. And if I take cold, it is only slight and doesn't stay with me very long and it doesn't make me sick either. I take other vitamins too, but just can't give enough credit to this priceless vitamin A.

I had carried a nagging cold on and off for quite a few years.

I took cold tablets and many antihistamines, yet it still plagued me, especially in school, and left me miserable at night. Then I read an article, "Resistance Requires Vitamin A." Deciding I had nothing to lose and not really expecting much, I started taking fish-liver oil every day along with a few other natural foods with vitamin A. Now, three weeks later, I hardly have even a sniffle.

I'm looking for the best in nutrition for my family, as it helps me so much. I'm a homemaker and I want to be the best. A good diet at home makes for a great deal of kindness and joy.

I've tried this for the first signs of a cold and it works too: four vitamin C tables (100 mg.), one dolomite tablet, followed in one hour with three vitamin C; at the end of another hour take two more vitamin C and one dolomite, and then one vitamin C tablet each hour for a day, when all signs of a cold are gone.

Our neighbors had colds that developed into the Hong Kong flu, but not us.

On Colitis

My most distressing health problem was diagnosed as colitis. I was eating the usual American diet of sterilized milk, artificial foods, white bread, polished rice, butter, precooked vegetables, and excessive quantities of refined sugar in the form of candy, sweetened beverages, and ice cream. My doctor, however, insisted I give up only cereals, flour, macaroni, bran, spaghetti, bread, crackers, and the like. He explained that, in patients with colitis, food goes rapidly through the upper or small intestine, which does not allow time for proper digestion. I found his prescribed diet, while bland, was irritating my colon.

I felt this would leave me starving until I learned what I could substitute in its place. However, I was helped by eating ripe bananas, which have vitamins B and B₂ (riboflavin), some A and C, as well as minerals, and have easily assimilable sugars. To this I added foods such as brewers' yeast and wheat germ, rich in B vitamins. In ten days my condition improved.

I lost my husband nearly a year ago. He had been ill for two years. Since his death, I often wonder if he would still be with me today if I could have convinced him that his foolish eating habits, which he refused to change, were the cause of his colitis.

He lived on carbohydrates; I avoided them like the plague. He was chronically tired; for me, there were not enough hours in the day for all the things I wanted to do for him and others.

I tried to replace white rice with brown rice, to give him fresh fruits and vegetables; to have honey and molasses take the place of the sugar he consumed in his strong tea and coffee. The excessive amount of salt and seasoning which I left out and he added were only a few of his food indiscretions. The others are too numerous to mention.

After his death, I returned to my volunteer and church work, and I was surprised to find that two close women friends of mine had operations for colon problems due to colitis. One has been ill more than a year and the second is now in her seventh week in the hospital with complications resulting from the operation. Their food choices when I joined them at luncheon or dinner were excessive carbohydrates. Their dessert was ice cream with fudge or chocolate sauce. They turned a deaf ear to my suggestions about their nutrition. They envied my get up and go, but would not heed my advice.

It has been my belief, confirmed by health literature, that years on a high-carbohydrate diet may in fact be responsible for the recent increase in colitis cases, spastic colon, and more serious rectal and colon problems. If an operation is not imperative (because of an obstruction), I would vote first for putting the patient on a low-carbohy-three weeks.

I have been suffering for years with gas, acidity, and constipation, which led to spastic colitis. My doctor advised an operation. I refused to go to the hospital and struggled along with different remedies, but to no avail.

I have been learning about nutrition and following the rules. I am delighted with the change in my health. I discovered I was eating wrong, too much bread for one thing, and not enough fruits and vegetables. I could not eat meat. Thanks to wonderful nutrition books, my acidity and gastric attacks are disappearing. I have no ill effects after a meal, neither do I worry about what I should eat. My hunger pangs also have disappeared. What I have learned, I have been telling my friends.

On Diabetes

There is no greater shock than to learn that you have diabetes. That there are 4 million diabetics and 10 million pre-diabetics in America does not help make me feel better, but it is a sad commentary that the physicians today cannot stop this epidemic.

My first lesson was to learn where and how I could get

natural poison-free food grown on fertile soil. It was to be eaten either fresh or not overcooked. I had to learn to avoid all foods that contain refined salt, hydrogen and fats, white flour, white sugar, and glucose and dry cereals. I was to use kelp in place of salt, natural cold-pressed oils, whole-grain cereals. I could eat a small amount of honey if it had not been pasteurized (for instance, tupelo honey from Florida). I made fresh fruits and vegetables a large part of my diet, and nuts and seeds my midafternoon snacks. I had an occasional baked potato but never ate creamed or fried potatoes, as I was watching my weight and they were forbidden.

All this together with my vitamin supplements help me to keep insulin and medication to a minimum.

My husband and I have been on a "health kick" since the days of the older nutritionists, going back some twenty-five years. We started using daily doses of the B vitamins and just about all the other vitamin and mineral supplements as they became known, and followed a good food regimen.

I show no trace of diabetes, although my father, mother, brother, sister all died of diabetes respectively at ages seventy-four, eighty-five, forty, fifty-three. All of us had a passion for sweets and starches—only I suppressed it. At age sixty-eight my blood pressure is that of a thirty-five-year-old. This, I believe, is due to my early interest in nutrition.

On the Ears

My problems were tinnitus (ringing and noises in the ear), restless legs at night, and general fatigue. I was given tranquilizers to quiet my legs and told I would have to accept the ear problem, as nothing could be done to alleviate it. Fortunately, I was sent to a physician who was interested in what I was eating. He had a long chart which I filled out carefully and returned to him on my next visit. I received a diet sheet that I was told to follow explicitly. My diet had been particularly bad because I travel with my husband and we live in hotels, without facilities for real cooking. I used convenience foods when we did not eat in restaurants.

I knew it would take ingenuity and fortitude to be able to follow this new way of living. The doctor said it would be a real challenge but once I mastered it, it would not be too difficult.

I shall mention a few of his suggestions: lecithin granules were suggested for low energy and cholesterol; vitamin B complex, with emphasis on niacin; also vitamins A, C, E, and B_6, and potassium; whole grain bread; unsaturated fats; and fresh foods to replace canned foods; and I switched from sugar to honey and molasses.

Within six months the ear problem lessened and the restlessness in my legs cleared completely, giving me additional rest because of more peaceful sleep.

When one really learns how to use nutrition, it is like becoming acquainted with a whole new world.

On Epilepsy (Petit Mal)

Vitamin therapy as a method of treatment for epilepsy actually is still in an experimental stage. But it cannot do harm and often it is helpful.

Studies indicate that families in which several members suffer from chronic diseases seem to have unusually high needs for certain vitamins because the members of these families have often followed, perhaps for generations, the same vitamin-deficient diet. Unfortunately, many of these people know all too little about the proper feeding of children and themselves. There was the case of an infant formula so deficient in vitamin B6 that it caused babies to suffer epileptic seizures, and the seizures ceased when B6 was added to the formula. If a formula that lacks one vitamin could have such a drastic effect, it is possible that the lack of other necessary vitamins and minerals could be the cause of many other problems.

A good neighbor told me about the use of vitamin E for a heart condition and epilepsy. I sent for some vitamin E capsules and started to give them to my grandson, who has epilepsy, and the benefit he has gotten is remarkable and should be mentioned to others. His epilepsy seizures diminished and he has lost excess weight but seems to have more energy.

I have read many articles concerning tests on persons with epilepsy. I am now fifty years of age and have suffered from this since I was seventeen years old. I went to dozens of doctors and had EEG tests with no resulting benefits. I tried several drugs and at last had my seizures reduced by one of them. But still I was always tense and nervous, and lived in constant fear of the next attack.

In an article that I read, it said that magnesium from dolomite had been helpful in many cases of epilepsy, and I started taking two tablets a day with my regular medication. I am happy to say that I have not had one petit mal attack in eighteen months.

I must have looked like a walking corpse before I started following food-for-health programs. I now take brewers' yeast, desiccated liver, vitamin C and E for circulation, and dolomite for magnesium. Now I am starting to live my next fifty years—I work as a nurse's aide and have raised two children.

There has been much research on diet in relation to epilepsy. This was thought to be incurable, with anticonvulsion drugs the only answer.

When I began to investigate what had been done, I learned that a diet of low carbohydrates, high protein, and the proper amount of fat and supplements had shown great improvement in many sufferers. Seizures were reduced greatly. My own results seemed to depend upon how carefully I adhered to the diet. When I became careless, I noticed that it was particularly the carbohydrates that brought on the attacks, especially when I did not get enough protein. I rode this merry-go-round until I was convinced this had to be a new way of life for me. I had to pass up the ice cream and salted pretzels which were my afternoon companions as I sat in the park to study.

In place of these snacks I learned to take high-protein tablets and brewers' yeast tablets, with emphasis on vitamin B_6. I have become calmer and able to cope with many problems which seemed insurmountable before I changed my diet. I hope eventually the cause of epilepsy will be found and that many more people will be helped. In the meantime, I would suggest to those needing help that magnesium oxide is also important with vitamin B_6.

I feel I must tell what an answer to prayers B_6 (pyridoxine) was for my epileptic child.

I want to encourage other mothers to investigate nutrition and try it! We had to find something harmless and natural. I put 2 tablespoons of brewers' yeast a day in my baby's bottle, and within a few days, he showed improvement. I also gave him 10-milligram tablets of B₆ daily, and his night twitching stopped.

Our young son, who suffered epileptic seizures for three years (despite conventional anti-convulsant therapy), was not relieved until we followed the suggestion in an article that mentioned vitamin B₆ as a help in some types of seizures. It worked. One week after administering B₆, our boy was seizure free, and has remained so for one year.

On Estrogenic Hormones

As a follower of a fairly good food program, I feel in good condition at age fifty-five. I had little or no discomfort during menopause, so I was surprised when I was informed that my estrogen was low. The doctor suggested that I take estrogenic hormones, by injection or orally; otherwise, he said, bones become weak and brittle.

I am adverse to this kind of medication as I do not like to suppress the natural function of the ovaries. I began to check on my nutrients and minerals and vitamin E. I concentrated on enriching my cooking with extra wheat germ and sunflower meal, and adding brewer's yeast in my drinks and soups. On my next examination my hormone balance was normal.

Nutrition may not be considered an aid to medical problems, but it has helped me enormously.

On the Eyes

An opthalmologist (a medical doctor specializing in eyes), can, by examination, detect a vitamin A deficiency, which is a cause of night blindness, in your system. He can also detect early signs of cataract or glaucoma. As a matter of fact, the general state of your health can be determined through examination of the eyes.

There is a growing accumulation of evidence that vitamin B₂ (riboflavin) is necessary for the health of the eye. In experiments with rats, chickens, and monkeys that were fed a diet deficient in riboflavin, cataracts developed. The addition of vitamin B₂ to the diet will not repair the damage that has already occurred, but it does deter the further progress of the cataract. Cataracts usually start in one eye, and it is of the utmost importance that a proper nutritional program be followed to prevent the onset of a cataract in the other eye.

Sufficient B₂ in the diet also is helpful in cases of failing vision, or of a burning sensation and in excessive watering of the eyes. Vitamins A₁ and B₂ also are helpful for conjunctivitis.

The natural foods most important for eye health are carrots, tomatoes, sweet potatoes, green leafy vegetables, parsley, sunflower seeds, and brewers' yeast.

I have had some marvelous experiences with health foods and supplements since I became interested in the subject of natural cures a few years ago. My first experience started with my youngest son, who had sun blindness so badly that he could not enjoy the summer. I put him on 20,000 units of carrot oil (vitamin A), and in three months all sign of sun blindness was gone. I have kept him on 10,000 units from that time on, and the condition has not returned.

I've found by trial and experiment that all vitamins are essential. But one especially I have in mind is vitamin C. I take anywhere from 60 to 120 times the minimum daily requirement. It helps my eyes wonderfully. If I fall below 40 times the minimum, then I don't see as well.

I am seventy-four year old, and before I started the vitamin C supplement I was having quite a bit of trouble with my eyes. I do very strenuous physical labor, yet many young men I work with cannot keep up with me. I recently started night school, going three nights a week.

For many years I have been troubled with conjunctivitis. There is a definite way of improving this bothersome condition. I experienced with increased vitamin A and D intake this spring, when itchy, bloodshot, and watery eyes were driving me crazy. As long as I can remember I used eyedrops and drugstore vitamins A and D. When I learned about natural vitamins, I obtained natural and more potent ones.

On reading Dr. [Linus] Pauling's book [on vitamin C], I increased my vitamin C intake to 3,000 milligrams per day in anticipation of my yearly hay fever, which I have had regularly from the middle of August till after the first frost every year.

The result of my new knowledge enabled me to discard the eyedrops, since the itching, watering, and redness soon disappeared. When the time of my usual hay fever suffering approached, I had a few sniffles and sneezes, but I took the precaution of carrying my vitamin C with me and taking it around the clock at the sign of the slightest symptom. I was completely free of this plague for the rest of the season.

I have continued on my nutritional program, for the combined high dosages of A, D, and C performed a true miracle for me.

From earliest childhood I had to wear glasses for nearsightedness, and for a boy this was a great handicap because it limited sports activity. Added to that, there was also the taunting of some stupid classmates.

It was not until much later in life that I learned that vision is directly linked to nutrition, that a poor diet can mean poor eyesight. There is evidence that, even in affluent societies, preventable defects of vision are much too frequent. Faulty or inadequate nutrition can have its deleterious effects at any time of life, but particularly as one gets older. Lack of vitamins and other elements and lack of protein, together with resulting imbalances in my system, had led to my faulty vision.

I learned that the way to avoid sight problems is to eat a well-balanced diet rich in liver, fish, milk, eggs, watercress, parsley, endive, carrots, apricots, and tomatoes, with brewers' yeast and wheat germ for B complex added. My eyesight improved gradually. Taking vitamin A for night blindness corrected that problem.

But I was concerned about the degeneration of the retina and the possibility of cataracts at my advanced age (middle seventies). I read that several physicians abroad (in Italy) had done research work on this problem with vitamin E, prescribing 600 milligrams a day. The majority of their patients showed marked improvement in the eye tissue and muscle. I had been taking 200 units as part of my new routine. I have increased it to 600 milligrams.

It is too soon to tell final results, but I know that my general health is better and that this nutritional buildup is helping my eyes.

On Fatigue

For many of you, the day now starts with artificial orange juice, instant waffle mix, instant pancake mix, or instant oat-

meal, and concludes with instant coffee, with, perhaps, a nondairy cream taking the place of real cream or milk. Or you may take, in place of these, a whole "instant breakfast." Instant mashed potatoes, puddings, and cake mixes are probably also on your menus.

If you read the labels on these "instant" products and add up the preservatives and chemicals (instead of natural foods) you are putting into your body each day, you will find they constitute a potential danger because they lack the vitamins and minerals that are so vitally needed by your body.

Our country is considered the best fed in the world, but because of the use of huge amounts of refined, devitalized, and demineralized foods, there is evidence of indisputable general malnutrition among its people.

If you are not yet one of the 67 million Americans suffering from diabetes, arteriosclerosis, arthritis or hypoglycemia, you have a constitution which is a little tougher than others. These 67 million people feel miserable, fatigued, often too weak to open all the boxes and cans of instant food they use, and take extra drinks before and after dinner to lift their spirits.

We were a group of professors who were frankly in poor physical shape. One of the professors' wives had become interested in nutrition and suggested we start an experiment. Since we were just getting through our regular day's work, we all decided to participate. We started with 1 teaspoon of concentrated wheat-germ oil taken in conjunction with increasing amount of exercise. Within a short time we found this improved our endurance.

We learned honey is popular among athletes as an energy producer, for it has a rich supply of dextrose that sends it to the liver to be turned into glycogen. We used 2 tablespoons of honey (unpasteurized) thirty minutes before exercises.

At mealtime we ate an increased amount of high protein, mainly lean meat and fish, and organ meats for B vitamins. We increased our intake of fresh fruits and vegetables for vitamin C. Our supplements were brewers' yeast, desiccated liver, rose hips for additional vitamin C, wheat germ, and wheat-germ oil plus vitamin E. For quick energy between classes we depended on nuts and raisins.

We lost weight, our energy increased, and by focusing our health program on improved nutrition, we are no longer exhausted and devoid of energy at the end of the day.

We always laughed at my aunt. She did such odd things, like making us drink nutritious milk and eat unpeeled vegetables. Why, she even made piecrust with whole wheat flour!

When she gave me several books by well-known nutritionists, I really did think she was carrying things a bit too far. But after I had two children within two years' time, I wondered if all her healthful living had made the woman psychic.

Marriage and two babies were a terrible adjustment for me to make in such a short while. Because I was so busy, I prepared mostly instant and canned foods. I was always tired, so I drank coffee continuously for the lift it gave me, smoking at least two cigarettes with each cupful. And I always had candy in the house for quick energy. I looked haggard, my eyes tired, my hair thin, dull, and lifeless. I had to keep taking in my clothes. When I awoke each morning, I felt glued to the bed, and my nerves were about to get the best of me.

Finally, I did go to an M.D. He tested my hemoglobin and told me I was fine. He did say that if it would make me feel better, I could go to the drugstore and buy a bottle of vitamins. I asked him what he thought about health foods, and he laughed. "Nothing but quackery," he said.

Still, I couldn't help thinking about how vibrant and young my aunt looked, and I decided to try it her way for a while. As a beginning, I went to the health-food store and bought my vitamins and a whole-wheat-bread mix. Then I went to the library and checked out several books written by "conforming" nutritionists. I was shocked to learn that the average American diet is deficient in many important vitamins, especially vitamin E and the B vitamins, which are destroyed when wheat is converted into white, bleached flour. Most of the food we eat is completely devitalized as a result of overprocessing.

Gradually, I changed my eating habits and those of my family. I began cooking with safflower oil instead of animal fat, and eating fresh fruit and vegetables daily. I baked whole wheat bread once a week, and soon our favorite "treat" was warm, oven-fresh whole wheat bread dripping with honey and butter. We switched to raw certified milk, and I started adding brewers' yeast to my babies' bottles. I even learned to sprout mung beans, and discovered that they gave scrambled eggs an exotic, Oriental flavor. I began taking cod liver oil daily. It did wonders for my skin and hair. Instead of candy bars and soft drinks, we snacked on dried fruits, nuts, and juices.

It didn't happen overnight, but in time there was a marked change for the better in my appearance, outlook, and feeling of well being. My willpower even increased to the point where I was able to cut out cigarettes and coffee, and I no longer woke up as tired as when I went to bed. It was amazing!

I raise an organic garden each year, and feel contempt for all of the lifeless, instant, overprocessed food constantly being thown at the public.

Our son was five months old when I registered for a course

in natural foods at a "free school" in our area. The catalog said the course was of "special interest to mothers of young children." Naturally, I wanted the best for my son. I didn't anticipate how much of what I would learn would apply to me.

I knew new mothers were often tired, but even after five months, just getting through each day was still an effort. At dinnertime, I always had a gin and tonic to help me relax. This left me feeling fuzzy and sleepy, and so, shortly after supper, I would go to bed.

My life seemed rather pointless, especially as I couldn't really enjoy my child as much as I wanted to. I dreaded the late afternoon feeding, when I would have to try to spoon the baby food into his unwilling little mouth. Little did I know how right his instincts were, how overprocessing had robbed his food of valuable vitamins and minerals, leaving a tasteless mush. No wonder he refused it. And he was always cranky. I blamed it on his teething and gave him teething biscuits made of white flour and white sugar, which only aggravated the real problem.

In the class, I learned about brewers' yeast and how the B vitamins it contained so plentifully would give me more energy. I also learned how coffee and alcohol destroyed these vitamins in our bodies. We started taking the yeast a little at a time to get used to its flavor. Right away we noticed a difference in the way we felt. I stopped having my nightly drink. My husband, who works nights, was able to stop drinking the many cups of coffee that a newspaper reporter traditionally has. But the best change was on our son, Jesse. His crankiness gave way to a sunny disposition, and for the first time in months he started sleeping through the night.

This inspired us to give up all white flour and white sugar—two notoriously "fake" foods robbed of their natural nutrients and B vitamins. As our bodies began getting the vitamins we needed, my "chronic" digestion problem cleared up, and my husband's red, bloodshot eyes were clear again. I wanted to call the eye doctor who had told my husband he would have to use eyedrops for the rest of his life. "Some people would says it's a lack of vitamins," he had told us, "but I don't agree."

Soon we had changed our diets almost completely to natural foods, including natural vitamins from my health-food store. This was especially important, as I was expecting my second child and planned to nurse it. I felt wonderful throughout my pregnancy and had a beautiful, healthy daughter.

The best discovery was how much better "real" foods taste. Our friends marvel at the taste of our milk—certified raw, of course. Those who are afraid of "catching something" from it we tell how much healthier it is. Some think natural foods are too expensive. I explain that although prices for them are sometimes higher, it is worth the extra expense to keep my family in good health. Besides, I discovered that when I stopped buying empty foods (potato chips, soda pop, cookies, and so-called convenience foods) in the super-market, my total grocery bill wasn't really any higher.

My son is nearly two now. The other mothers in the playground always comment on how strong and active he is. He does seem more coordinated than the other children his age, and he rarely catches the colds that are constantly making the rounds of his playmates. My friends say that I'm lucky he's so healthy. I wish I could convince them that good potluck comes from watching what goes into the pot.

When I was introduced to wholesome, nutritious food and learned the importance of vitamins and minerals in foods and the need for supplements, it made an enormous differ-ence in my life. The contrast can only be compared to changing living hell for serene contentment.

I finally became pregnant, to the delight of my husband and myself, three years after marriage. It was not an uneventful pregnancy or delivery (I had a last-minute Caesarean) but the details are too lengthy and gruesome to relate. It is sufficient to say that a lack of nutritional guidance resulting in a gain of forty-five pounds was probably responsible for the start of the problem which followed.

My own naivete and ignorance of the principles of good nutrition did not help the situation. That the child and I survived I can only attribute to our strong constitutions and heredity.

My second pregnancy followed nine months later. This time I gained only nineteen pounds and had a normal delivery. I was not encouraged to nurse either child, nor did I have the milk or strength to do so.

After the birth of my second child, I could not regain my strength. I was chronically fatigued and could not meet the challenges of the day. The pains and aches, low backache, and gallbladder disturbances made it difficult for me to face each day. After several years in and out of hospitals for checkups and evaluations, I fortunately escaped all the suggested operations—appendix, thyroid, gallbladder, and hysterectomy—yet I knew something had gone out of me with the birth of the second child and had to be replaced. But what?

We ate the same food as the average family. Juice, eggs, white toast, and plenty of coffee with sugar for breakfast. Lunch at home consisted for me of what the children left on their plates, or a salad and sandwich and more coffee. Dinner was a fruit cup or soup; meat, potatoes or some other starch, and a green vegetable or salad; followed by my husband's favorite apple pie and ice cream or cheesecake and more coffee. My midday snack was a Danish or doughnut or something else sweet that I thought would give me what energy I needed.

My winter colds and the sinus attacks that followed continued unabated. The arthritic-type pains in my shoulder and the backaches continued relentlessly, as did the fatigue, the lack of interest in sex, and the crying spells without provocation.

One young physician to whom I had mentioned my symptoms suggested I might have an estrogenic-hormone deficiency (at that time generally associated only with menopause and not suspected in younger women), stemming from the closeness of the births of my two children. I took the estrogen injections and pills he gave me, and they perked me up immeasurably. This doctor was the first I met who had some understanding of my hormone-deficiency problem. While I was soon feeling much better as a result of his treatment, I knew and felt something else was still lacking in me. Unfortunately, not much was known or understood then about vitamin deficiencies.

Vitamins in foods and their uses as medicines were just beginning to be recognized at this time (more than thirty years ago). Dr. Henry C. Sherman was then working at Columbia University on research in vitamin C and vitamin A. Vitamin A was being used for skin and hair problems by a dermatologist who treated my husband, with good results. Research was also being done on the B vitamins, and a Dr. Brady had a syndicated column suggesting uses for B vitamins.

My husband suggested that I look into the question of vitamins. It was then that I really became earnest in my search for more knowledge about nutrition.

I wrote to various universities and also to the government, for food charts on vitamins. Through this research I discovered that wheat germ and brewers' yeast were excellent sources of vitamin B complex and protein, that fish-liver oils supplied vitamin A and D, and that fresh fruits and vegetables were excellent for vitamin C and for supplements.

Giving up coffee was the most difficult thing I had to do, as it always is for cigarette smokers, but it can be done. It is now ten years since I have had coffee, and I don't miss it!

I am now in my mid-sixties and my husband is in his early seventies. We have grown children and grandchildren, and we are enjoying better health than we did thirty-five years ago.

Once, when I was home from college for the Christmas holiday, I stood before my mother's table and wondered at the differences (in color, texture, and aroma) between the foods on it and those I normally ate at school.

It occurred to me that I always felt less fatigued and seemed more alert after only a short holiday visit at home. I wondered if it could have anything to do with the food they served at school and my between-meal snacking.

I decided to investigate this possibility further. I felt it was as important to me as anything in my curriculum, especially if it helped me to keep well and able to do my assignments.

The first item I checked was bread. Mother still baked her own, and I questioned her as to the ingredients. They were wheat germ, whole grain, and brewers' yeast, as well as honey and oil and milk. While I could not bake or obtain such bread at school, I might be able to use some of the same ingredients. I decided they might make an interesting cereal, so I bought them from the health-food store mother patronized and took them back with me.

While I was shopping, I noticed some health-food books, and decided these might give me additional clues as to what I was doing right and what mistakes I was making. Now my quest had become an adventure. The recommendation these books made for cutting down on or for eliminating sugar altogether was the most difficult for me to follow, but I found that unsulfured California raisins and dried apricots as well as carob (St. John's bread) and other sweets made of honey and sesame satisfied my craving. Next, I checked the various nuts and seeds, such as pumpkin and sunflower, and added these to my snacks.

It is now six months since I started my new program of eliminating junk foods. I was amazed to find that during exams I didn't need coffee or Cokes with their overstimulating effect to keep me going. Another dividend has been my ability to get up early enough in the morning to enjoy my new breakfast and get in some exercise.

My weight has now levelled off and is keeping steady, which I assume is due to the elimination of my large intake of sugar. My friends and classmates have noticed my new energy, but have not yet taken the plunge themselves. Perhaps a book like this one will convince them to try my program, especially when they learn that poor nutrition can be a forerunner to a prediabetic condition and many other illnesses.

On Foot and Leg Problems

I have long had restless legs and a queer feeling in my feet, as if they did not belong to me. I was told the cause was poor circulation, but this explanation did not help me.

I have been careful with my diet—I eat no white sugar or white-flour products or ice cream. Nevertheless, the condition continued. The doctor said I could have circulatory polyneuritis or an allergy, but could offer no definite help. A friend sent me some information which suggested that in a case similar to mine, the treatment was vitamin B complex and vitamin B_6 (pyridoxine)—50 milligrams taken three times a day. I also took vitamin B_2, (25 milligrams); and for my circulation, vitamin E in large doses was suggested. I started with 400 milligrams.

It never occurred to me that my problem could be some sort of nutritional imbalance. I shall continue with these vitamin additions, as I feel much improved.

My grandmother never knew about vitamins and minerals and lived to be a hearty ninety. Back around the turn of the century, before the days of dieting and before foods were tampered with, many of our present-day illnesses were unknown. If heredity has anything to do with health, why didn't I inherit some of her vitality? Why did I have leg cramps at night, aches and pains in the morning, depression, and weeping spells at the slightest provocation, as well as other chronic ailments?

The doctors I had consulted had found nothing seriously wrong with me, and said many of my complaints were due to the pace of life. They said nothing about my eating patterns and diet habits. An article I read in a health magazine was the first clue to my many complaints. I decided that either my gourmet cooking would have to go or I would go the way of all flesh. No more pancakes and syrup with bacon and sausage for breakfast, no more coffee or strong tea and sugar. No cornflakes—they were to be replaced with whole-grain cereals and wheat germ. I also took brewers' yeast, extra vitamins, such as vitamin E and B_6 (for my leg cramps), and mineral supplements.

With my new health program, I hope to live to see the year 2000 come in!

In an automobile accident years ago, my left leg was badly damaged—tendons torn and veins and arteries crushed, forever after impairing circulation. Several years ago I began to suffer severe leg cramps that were so excruciating I would almost scream with pain. I was already taking multiple vitamins, and I increased the dosage of vitamin E to 700 milligrams daily, taken before meals, throughout the day. The cramping ceased. To check this out, I stopped the vitamin E for a while. Result: cramping returned.

While playing football in college, I injured both knees and my back but the injuries were neglected. Result: over the years, great discomfort and a substantial loss of mobility, especially in the knees. Then along came the information in Dr. [John] Ellis's book *[The Doctor Who Looked at Hands]* and your suggestion that I read about vitamin B6 in it. I followed Dr. Ellis's suggestions and within a week noticed a decrease in discomfort and an increase in mobility. This improvement has continued until the present. I am now almost completely free of discomfort and have regained a great deal of mobility. My back has also improved, but not at the same rate. I suppose this is due to the fact that I fractured a vertebra. I am happy to have you present my experience and hope it will help others to help themselves.

It was a lucky evening for me when we were seated together at Jeanie's party. I mentioned the problem with my leg so you would understand why I refused to dance. My leg had been numb and painful for nearly seven months. After seeing many doctors and trying many suggestions, I was finally reconciled to having an operation and the date was set for the following month.

When you asked me whether I would "like to try nutrition," it was not entirely clear to me what you meant, for you also suggested that I give up cigarettes, coffee, and all empty calorie foods, and add supplements and increased protein to my diet.

Your suggestion that I read Dr. John B. Ellis's book *The Doctor Who Looked at Hands* amused me, because mine was a leg problem. But I did read it. The book, describing so much research on hands and legs, suggests taking 50 milligrams a day of vitamin B6. In later research, the amount was raised. I decided to try this new approach to my problem. You assured me that nutrition would make me feel better even if it did not help my leg.

I was amazed that in only a few days I felt some movement in my toes. I thought first it was my imagination but I was encouraged to continue the B6, the vitamin supplements, and the improved diet.

After three weeks, I was walking and dancing. I telephoned the doctor and postponed the proposed surgery. I am much encouraged with the wonderful progress. I want to thank you for your wonderful suggestions.

A physician friend of mine related his experience to me. Since I had a similar problem I thought it would interest others.

"For many years I had been suffering with leg cramps at night," he said. I had discussed this with several of my colleagues. They were not familiar with any nutritional aids or vitamins for this most painful condition.

"While I am familiar with vitamin therapy in dermatology and other specialties, it was not until I read a research paper by a California physician that I learned that he had used vitamin E in his research. He had many patients report that they had used 800 units of vitamin E daily and the pains had been greatly alleviated."

My own experience had been similar, but I found relief

with vitamin B₆, other vitamins and minerals, and calcium from bone meal. I asked the doctor where he obtained his vitamins and whether they were natural or the drugstore variety. He obtained his from the pharmacy. I explained that vitamin B_6 costs three times as much from the pharmacy as from the health-food stores.

Many physicians are still prescribing 3-gram quinine tablets for leg cramps, and although they do help temporarily, many people have side effects from quinine. I have found it better to use the nutritional way wherever possible.

On a recent trip abroad, I had an unusual experience.

The approach to the top of Zante, one of the Ionian Islands, off Greece, is by donkey. On the day of our trip it rained and the road was very slippery, so we decided to walk back down the steep incline, the equivalent of twenty-seven flights of stairs. When we reached the bottom, my calves were aching. I did not have an opportunity to rest before we continued our sightseeing on the beautiful island of Rhodes, and I knew then that I was in serious trouble, for my legs were swollen to twice their normal size.

From Greece we went on to Yugoslavia, and at a clinic there I was able to see an orthopedic specialist. He informed me that I had a form of edema. He bandaged my legs tightly and told me to keep them elevated, and he advised against my walking at all for forty-eight hours. He also said I would be somewhat incapacitated for another five days, and that I would probably have pain and discomfort for three weeks, which was the earliest date I could expect complete healing.

When I returned to the hotel, I decided I had to do something nutritionally to try to speed the healing, for I had to get well quickly or cancel the remainder of the trip.

We have been following a full nutrition and vitamin

supplement regimen for the last twenty years and never travel without my health foods and vitamins. I decided to try vitamin B₆ and vitamin C, as both are advised by Dr. John M. Ellis for edema, and Dr. Linus Pauling advises vitamin C in megavitamin doses.

I took 400 milligrams of B₆ and 3,000 of vitamin C for two days, and then cut back to 150 milligrams vitamin B₆ and 1,000 of C.

The second time I saw the doctor, he was surprised at the improvement in the swelling. My husband suggested I explain the vitamin therapy to the doctor, but I decided it would be too difficult because of the language differences. In any event, after forty-eight hours my legs were back to normal and I did not have any of the discomfort the doctor had predicted. I attributed my complete and rapid recovery to the prompt use of both vitamin B₆ and vitamin C.

Dr. Ellis has written on the subject of edema in pregnancy, advising 450 milligramss of B₆, and Dr. Pauling has advised taking large doses of C after strenuous exercise, to relieve strained muscles.

I am seventy-two years of age and follow this health program: I take bone-meal tablets three days a week to prevent cavities in my teeth and also prevent cramps in my legs. When I do get leg cramps, I know there is not enough calcium in my system. Then I take one tablet of dolomite and one of bone meal after each evening meal, for three days. I also take one vitamin A (cod liver oil) capsule, one vitamin C (rose hips), two brewers' yeast (vitamin B), one vitamin E (vegetable oil) for a full week—seven days— preferably after the evening meal.

My husband has had phlebitis. He had seen several physicians and all prescribed a blood thinner, which did very little for him. I began to look for answers elsewhere. In a book by Dr. Wilfred Shute, *Vitamin E for Ailing and Healthy Hearts*, the author stated that "alpha-tocopherol was reported to be the best preventative as well as treatment for dissolving and removing freshly formed thrombi in the large veins of the legs." We decided that vitamin E (alpha-tocopherol) might be a happier and safer answer than blood thinners, since the book stated that, in larger doses, it not only prevents clots from spreading but also often melts them away rapidly.

I have kept him on good nutritious foods, vitamins, and minerals, and have now added vitamin B to these. It is truly amazing how much this therapy has helped this chronic case.

On the Gallbladder

I received a letter from my father in Germany that my mother was in the hospital there with a gallbladder attack. I was so worried I wanted to take the next flight to her. Then I remembered that several of my friends had told me that a doctor had suggested fasting and an apple-juice diet. I telephoned the information on this to my father, who suggested it to my mother's physician. He agreed to try it since he felt it could do no harm and he did not think her condition required an operation. The treatment was carried out in the hospital with excellent results and mother was home a few days later.

Here are the instructions for the apple-juice diet I sent along:

GALLBLADDER DIET

1. Drink one glass of apple juice every two hours for two days; eat nothing solid.

2. At the end of each day take one ounce of olive oil mixed with one ounce of apple juice, drinking it while lying on the right side. Remain in that position for one-half hour before going to sleep.

3. At the end of the second day, after taking the half-and-half mixture (of apple juice and olive oil), and after having lain on the right side for one-half hour, arise and take one tablespoonful of Epsom salts in one-half cup of warm water.

4. After the second day, avoid the following: all fats such as butter, margarine, mayonnaise, gravies, salad dressings; all fried foods; eggs; all dairy products. Eat only baked, roasted, or broiled meats, with all excess fat removed.

On Geriatrics

SCIENCE HAS FEW CURES FOR ILLS OF THE AGED *was the heading of a recent newspaper article. Another newspaper, however carried an article stating that "with proper nutrition, middle aged and after can be the vintage years."*

With nutrition, the scars of the past may not be eradicated, but at least the progress of deterioration may be slowed or even brought to a halt. The benefits resulting from a change in nutritional habits complemented by supplements and vitamins do not always show up as rapidly as some older persons expect they will, especially where there have been long-standing nutritional deficiencies. As a matter of fact, some deficiencies are irrevocable, yet, with patience, proper food, additional supplements, and megavitamin doses by injection, given under the supervision of a physician, such persons should certainly feel better.

Robert B. Choate startled the reading public when he said that most types of dry cereals have little nutritional value. This is of special interest to older persons who, lacking nutritional knowledge or cooking facilities—or even because they are denture wearers—often use cereals as a convenience food. However, wheat germ is a nutritious dry cereal if one avoids the overtoasted and oversweetened variety.

Keeping slim is imperative as one grows older. A proper low-fat diet with plenty of protein (meats, fish, eggs), fruits and vegetables, and with no white sugar and very little starch, is nature's key to good health and proper weight at any age.

My husband agreed to try a change of eating habits for a month. The hacking cough he had had for years disappeared —due no doubt, to the fact that, after "rolling his own" for sixty years, he no longer desired to smoke. There were no more dizzy spells, the ringing in his ears stopped, his eyes became clear and sparkling; he had no more headaches, upset stomach, constipation, or colds. His neck does not "crunch" any more when he turns his head, and he no longer needs to wear his glasses when he drives. It has always been hard for him to get up in the mornings. Now he is up at six or seven—and without a complaint! Instead of stooping, he now stands tall and straight.

Because of an accident in which he received four breaks in his back, doctors said he would never walk again. When I brought him home from the hospital, I fed him organically raised food and organic supplements, which we still take, and, with great determination, he walked a bit each day. Now, two years later, he does heavy physical work each and every day because he likes it. From 110 pounds he is back to his normal 165 pounds. He has made a 100 percent recovery—every break has knit perfectly.

I was, you see, one of those "good" cooks (I never realized I wasn't a healthy one). Our changeover has been simple. We discontinued using all white-flour products, all commercially canned foods, margarine, condiments, solid shortening, white sugar, salt, dry cereal, chocolate, and soft drinks. We use organically raised eggs, meat, fruit and vegetables, many of them raw, brown rice, carob flour, honey or raw sugar, cornmeal, brown rice flour and cold-pressed oil. We eat sunflower seeds each day and many nuts, use yeast instead of baking powder, only a small amount of organic whole-wheat flour, little milk, butter, cheese, and sea salt. To all my regular recipes I add such items as wheat germ, lecithin, bone meal, brewers' yeast, and dolomite.

Now our food is full of nutrients—and *far* superior in flavor. No longer do we need that between- or before-bedtime snack. We are completely content with our three simple meals a day.

At the age of eighty-seven, after one stroke, I learned how to grow younger. I began to eat mainly raw fruits, vegetables, nuts, hulled sunflower and pumpkin seeds, sprouted mung beans, alfalfa and wheat seeds, soaked chia seed, carob powder, comfrey leaves in salad and ground comfrey roots and flaxseed-meal tea, honey, and bee pollen. I took no white sugar, no white flour, no coffee, no tea, no chocolate, no tobacco, no alcohol, no aspirin, no sleeping pills.

I have read many books and periodicals that have taught me what I now know at age ninety. Among the unexpected benefits I received was help for my asthma, for which I can thank my physician, who thinks "food is your best medicine." He suggested that zucchini, string beans, celery, and parsley would help to eliminate my asthma. I think more people should have the benefits of comfrey and raw vegetables as I did.

I am not looking for publicity, only trying to battle malnutrition and pollution.

Seventeen years ago, when I was sixty, I was run down, nervous, irritable, and depressed, had poor eyesight, frequent colds, and was in a state of perpetual fatigue. I had never learned to drive and I was convinced I couldn't start at age sixty; I just knew I'd never pass the examination. I also wanted to teach school again. Once, long ago, I had taught, but that was before my first boy was born, more than forty years earlier. But time and life had flown swiftly by, and I suddenly realized that I wasn't much more than a candidate for the old-folks' home.

My husband and I had always lived on a farm and it had never occurred to us that we might be eating unhealthfully. What could be better for a person than good farm food? Plenty, I found out, if "farm food" meant hotcakes and syrup, chicken fried in lots of grease, mashed potatoes and gravy, and the home-baked pastry that is the pride of any farm wife.

One Christmas we visited some old friends and discovered that they were enthusiastic over something they called "health food." It sounded pretty peculiar to my husband and me; good food is good food, isn't it? They told us No; what we called "good food," they said, was actually very unhealthy. We would have dismissed the entire thing as crazy, but they were old friends and had never been known to go off the deep end. They told us that we would feel ever so much better if we ate as they did; they even came out and said we'd feel almost like youngsters again. Well, that was a little too far-out to accept, but my husband and I decided to anyway. We felt so allover awful, what did we have to lose?

It took a lot of willpower at first. No more greasy, high-carbohydrate foods; instead, lots of our farm vegetables, steamed with herbs, instead of boiled and dripping with butter; lots of lean beef broiled lightly, instead of fried in hard grease; and, most important of all, lots of organic supplements.

After about six months we did feel as if we were youngsters again. The chores were getting done with no trouble at all; my husband decided that there was no reason at all why I couldn't teach again, since I wanted to so badly. I've just gotten my new license after passing the examination with flying colors, and I drive twenty five miles to school each way every day.

I raise all my own fruits and vegetables in my own organic garden. This year I've got tomatoes, yams, Irish potatoes, corn, beans, cantaloupes, and casaba melons. Some years I put in watermelon and cucumbers, and many other vegetables. I alternate the kinds of vegetables because I freeze them for use in winter, and I don't like to eat exactly the same diet every year.

I wish that there were some way I could convey to people that being "old" is not a matter of age; it's a matter of outlook and bodily condition. Without health foods I'd probably be in some old-folks' home right now, instead of raising my own food, teaching school, driving, and redecorating my home. If I could show some older people how I myself was at sixty—run-down and ready to retire to the rocker—and how I am *myself* seventeen years later, teaching school and running with the children on the playground, perhaps they'd realize that they could do it too. All it takes is wanting to make it so.

My brother and his wife and my wife and I have been following a health regimen for two decades, and are now starting on a third. My brother is an octogenarian, and I am entering my seventh decade. Both of us, and our families as well, are enjoying much better health than before we began taking vitamins, minerals, and food supplements, and exercising regularly. The cumulative benefits of the regimen to each of us are little less than amazing. Our good health testifies to that. Both families praise the system. We are glad to join our neighbors and friends in the universal approval being given the system for better health. I should like to recount some of the specific instances when my wife and I benefited by taking vitamins, minerals, and supplements.

I take an average of eighteen of these several times a day; my wife takes a smaller number at the same time. Right now, we are recovering from severe winter colds after redoubling the dosage of vitamins A and C. My wife has taken nothing but vitamins for three colds this winter.

Our family doctor maintains large files labeled "vitamins" and "minerals." A few years back, I developed shingles and he gave me five injections of vitamin B_{12}. I have not been troubled with shingles since. I have had hay fever since the early thirties, but the attacks are now shorter and less intense than formerly. During my youth, my blood pressure was high, but it has been normal now for several years. My pulse is also normal. I believe certain of the vitamins and food supplements prevent the formation of excessive cholesterol deposits and have helped to keep my blood normal. We feel that vitamin B_6 and vitamin E have stopped cramps in our legs. Neither of us is troubled with rheumatism or arthritis.

All of us know how hard it is to reduce or even to maintain normal weight. I believe that a full complement of vitamins, minerals, and food supplements can help every overweight person bear his burden and help in the reduction!

I am now past ninety years of age and have unusually good health. I have a full head of hair, hear well, and do not need dentures. I still drive my car. I have been able to read extensively for the last nine years without glasses, even though I had worn them for the previous forty years. I corrected my vision, even at that late period in my life, by taking 50,000 to 75,000 units of vitamin A daily, and sometimes I read until after midnight.

I am a firm believer in the value of minerals and vitamins in my foods, and use only natural or complete foods, when I can obtain them. I eat oatmeal with plenty of wheat germ, blackstrap molasses topped off with 2 tablespoons of sunflower or pumpkin-seed meal (freshly ground), and skim milk; I take no sugar. I supplement this diet with vitamin A, B complex, 300 milligrams of vitamin C, 200 units of vitamin E, bone meal, dolomite and sea kelp tablets, and 2 eggs daily.

I am eighty years old, will be eighty-one in January. I eat good, sleep good, hear good, walk a mile or more when I want to. It pays to eat health foods. I do, and I feel good all the time. If we put anything into a car but gasoline, it won't run. If we eat all kinds of unhealthy foods, we won't run either.

Oh, yes, I forgot to say I do not smoke, do not drink, do not take dope, do not have any aspirin or other tablets in the house—I don't even use liniments or such.

I grind up carrots and green peppers and celery for my vitamin A and put them together, then add a little salad dressing, and that is my salad.

On Gout

As a long-time reporter for a weekly news magazine, I am a skeptic both by inclination and training.

The night my wife walked in to announce that a health-food store had opened in our Chicago suburb, I muttered something about "food fads" and refused to hear more about it.

Like a number of other persons, including not only journalists but even an increasing number of high-school students, I'm a victim of gout. The first medical specialist I visited told me that, contrary to the popular picture of gout as the disease of high-living rich, its chief victims are people who work under mental pressure.

It doesn't fit in with that old Katzenjammer image of a bandaged big toe and a choleric old gentleman with his foot up on a hassock. Gout can attack any or all joints of the body. It can erode them as much as arthritis erodes them. The pain can be excruciating. In fact, two researchers who injected themselves with uric acid derivatives to get a subjective reaction to a gout attack found the pain so bad that both almost blacked out and immediately gave up the subjective part of their experiment.

Gout has been known through antiquity. Ancient Viking burials have been found where the body joints were almost totally destroyed by recurring gout attacks. I'd already been through four doctors, two of them gout sufferers themselves. I'm familiar with all the antigout drugs, so perhaps I can be pardoned my supercilious snort when my wife ventured to suggest that nutrition could help me.

But if a thing hurts badly enough, you get desperate enough to try anything. I was desperate. My drug bill was up to fifty dollars some months. Worse, I seemed to be losing ground. My joints creaked with a sandpaper sound, even when I simply turned my head. My sport is swimming, but I was afraid to do much of it because I'd been told the shock of cold water can precipitate a gout attack.

I still didn't give in easily. Then my wife brought home

a book on nutrition from that new health store. I grumped through one chapter at my wife's insistence. By the time I finished it, I was hooked. I read far into the night about gout and about other diseases that could be checked with something as simple and wonderful as vitamins.

I bought other books. I began comparing vitamin preparations. I learned about the effectiveness of vitamin E in particular in checking gout symptoms. It all began to work.

Only if you've been through a gout attack or have hovered on the brink of such an attack for months can you appreciate the delight of dropping all gout medication for weeks at a time. My drug bills sank. My vitamin and supplemental food expenditures rose, but in no way could they compare with my previous drug bills. I discovered things like wheat germ and yogurt. To nutritionists, these may be old hat. To me, they were a new world of steadily widening dimensions.

Not only am I swimming again, but I passed the license exam for scuba instructor last year—the oldest student in the class! And this spring I dove 60 feet beneath Wisconsin lake ice in January and February, in water registering 36 degrees, when the air measured 20 degrees. Even in an insulating wet suit, that is no mean test of physical condition.

The summer had come and gone and it had left me with ten unwanted pounds. I decided to lose them quickly by injections and near starvation. While I accomplished the weight loss, I put myself in a tailspin of emotional upset and unaccountable aches and pains.

The doctor suggested a blood analysis and this showed a high uric acid level for the first time in my history. He suggested various pills for gout of the large toe, and even though he chose the mildest dosage, I did not react favorably to it. So I decided to do a little research myself on gout to see what effects nutrition or vitamins might have on it.

One nutrition book stated that overnight persons who fast without taking pantothenic acid can actually produce both arthritis and gout in themselves! The amount of pantothenic acid needed daily varies with the severity and number of stresses one is under. However, the vitamin B complex to which it belongs is never toxic, so I took 50 milligrams daily.

Dr. E. P. Ralli of New York University College of Medicine studied a group of young men under the stress of swimming in icy water, first when they had been given no pantothetic acid and again after they had received 10,000 milligrams daily of the vitamin containing it. The tests showed that the vitamin gave protection in dozens of ways, for instance, by preventing body proteins from being destroyed, blood sugar and blood pressure from dropping, and calcium from being stolen from the bones.

Persons usually recover more rapidly from arthritis or some other severe stress when they receive 50 to 100 milligrams of pantothenic acid after each meal, between meals, and before bed, always with an otherwise adequate diet. When stresses decrease, a daily dose of 100 milligrams or less may be adequate, especially if brewers' yeast (1 to 3 tablespoons), 2 tablespoons of wheat germ, and liver are included in the diet.

A large cherry intake has also been said to be effective in the treatment of gout and arthritis. Following this proposal, I found a concentrated cherry juice in the health-food store and used one teaspoon daily in juice diluted with water. I also purchased pantothenic-acid tablets and used 50 milligrams, twice daily. Vitamin E had been suggested for checking gout, so I increased my previous intake of 100 milligrams to 400 milligrams daily. There has been no recurrence of the attacks.

On the Hair

My hair had been falling out, I seemed to have aged, the corners of my mouth were sore, and the mucous colitis from which I suffered had not subsided. One of the first things I had decided to do, after reading health magazines, was to take a complete vitamin supplement, as it is difficult for someone living alone to have proper nourishing meals. At least, I don't seem to. Then I secured employment staying with an elderly convalescent, taking the night shift. This gave me regular hours, although not complete relaxation or rest. At 7.00 A.M. each morning you could find me walking to the bus. True, it was only a block, but the birds were singing, the sun was coming up, and it was nice. Then I had a little less than a block to walk when I got off the bus.

Although my hair is still thin, it is no longer falling out. Also, it seems to be getting darker, although the crown is still silver. Could the vitamins be doing that? People think me to be ten or fifteen years younger than I am (seventy-two). I still have a problem with the mucous colitis, but my mouth is healed.

It would be interesting to know if vitamins could have anything to do with hair coloration.

My husband's hair started to turn gray when he was around twenty years old. By the time he was thirty, it was all gray. For the past year or so we have been taking multiple vitamins (all natural, of course), plus bone meal, garlic, parsley, desiccated liver, lecithin, acerola, etc. This sounds unbelievable, I know, but my husband's hair is all growing in black again. Each time he gets a haircut, the barber is amazed. All the older men he works with want a list of the vitamins he is taking.

I used to have to coax and beg him to take his vitamins. Now, if I don't have them ready, he begs for them. He is fifty-seven years old, does hard labor, and says he couldn't do it without his "pills."

On Headaches

After my two older children had left for school, I sat alone at the kitchen table staring at my third cup of coffee. The dull insistent throb of a headache had been with me for as many mornings as I could remember.

The ring of the doorbell brought me out of my lethargy and the postman handed me a package. It was a health book from my sister. We had discussed what she called "health foods" but I was impervious to her suggestions; it all seemed too complicated. Didn't everyone eat convenience foods? A mother with four children must look for shortcuts.

I leaned back, exhausted, and stared at the book. I decided to scan it before the children returned. After reading the first chapter, it seemed too good to be true. Foods that could prevent cavities, runny noses and flu epidemics—and possibly my migraine headaches? Then and there I decided to give it a try.

My first purchases were bone-meal powder, which contained calcium, phosphorus and other minerals. This I blended with high-protein powder and skim-milk powder for the children's milk. To their cereal I added wheat germ. Incidentally, I added wheat germ even to the prepared baking mixes I resorted to occasionally. I also used it in meat loaf, which I made from beef, veal, pork, and any "innards" the butcher had on hand. I always kept carrots in the refrigerator for snacking, and likewise unpeeled cooked apples.

Gradually, as I gathered strength, the world began to look sunny. I became fascinated with the whole idea of checking every label for chemicals and food values; I looked for ways and means to enrich our foods. I kept records of food values: I compared white rice with brown, white sugar with honey and molasses, whole grain bread with white. I found after a few months that the savings in medical and dental bills more than made up for the little extras and the vitamin supplements I purchased.

Ever since I was ten years of age, when I had rheumatic fever, I have had migraine headaches, so severe at times that they put me to bed for two or three days. Doctors would give me strong drugs for relief, but none could suggest any way to prevent the migraines from occurring. I explored every lead I could get, but none worked. I even tried to follow a nutrition plan, but found out that if one misses one point, it throws the whole off.

Last summer I had a large garden in which I grew lots of vegetables, and we had fruit trees with a good yield in our yard. I ate my fill of tomatoes, cabbage, cucumbers, radishes, etc., and of the raw fruit from our trees. I had no headaches from July till Thanksgiving. Then, after the garden produce gave out, the headaches came again. I concluded that my system needed the raw vegetables for enzymes, minerals, and bulk. When I resumed eating vegetables with every meal, behold, my migraine headaches stopped. And twice a day I drank strong herb teas, not straining them, but also eating the grounds.

I am seventy-eight years old and my trouble is I get old too fast and learn too slow. I believe an old person should not die of disease; a person should just naturally wear out. It seems old people don't eat right; they eat sweets, drink coffee, cooked food, prepared foods.

After all these years, I am happy to know how to stop migraine headaches.

For months I had been incapacitated with chronic headache, dizziness, and extreme fatigue. My muscles were so weak I could not carry on normal activity and had difficulty in starting the business day. I made the usual rounds of doctors for examinations and tests, but they revealed no abnormalities. So, at age fifty, I was bedridden and forced to retire from a lucrative business. This gave me more time to read. An article about nutrition caught my attention, and through this I became aware that, if this article was correct, my diet had not been all it should be. I telephoned my doctor and asked him whether there were any vitamin and mineral tests which might find some deficiency that had been overlooked. He ordered a new battery of tests, and, much to our surprise, the laboratory reported I had a severe magnesium deficiency as well as other borderline deficiencies.

My doctor was as unprepared for this disclosure as I was and unfamiliar with the damage such "minor" deficiencies could cause, but said he would go into this further. Together we discovered that an inadequate diet can cause a magnesium deficiency, and this can mean the difference between health and severe illness. It had interfered with my normal muscle activity, upset my blood pressure, caused an unusual body odor, and other problems too numerous to mention.

While passing a health-food store near his office, he decided to inquire about magnesium supplements and obtained a book listing the foods containing the maximum amounts of magnesium. I thought it best to go into this study myself more thoroughly since I had some borderline deficiencies and my diet must have been very poor to bring me to such a state of debilitation. I am learning gradually that one does not have a single missing nutrient but a combination, as they exist in all foods, and we must eat a variety of the correct ones. My food habits have undergone a drastic change, but I don't miss the old ways. My headaches are gone!

I want to praise the efforts of those who educate people to maintain and enjoy good health.

I found sugar to be very harmful. I used to get terrible migraine headaches. After eliminating sugar for two years, I feel much more alert mentally and no longer have headaches and days of inactivity due to them. It is wonderful to wake up with a clear mind instead of feeling sluggish and headachy. When I eat anything with sugar in it, I get blemishes on my face and back within a few hours, and my headaches return.

My husband's history of suffering from duodenal ulcers has greatly improved since he too eliminated sugar from his diet and is taking vitamin E, vitamin C, all-day vitamin B, and a multiple vitamin, plus dolomite. We follow a balanced diet. We eat organically raised vegetables when we can get them, we use freshly ground flour to make our bread and baked desserts, fresh fruits for desserts, and eat an adequate daily quota of protein. We had no colds last year. We enjoy using millet for cereal and rose hips tea for a hot beverage.

My mother, who lives with us, has improved and maintained her health by watching her foods, as we do. She used to suffer terrible headaches and dizziness resulting from a slight diabetic condition. We have a lot to be thankful for. My mother is seventy-two years old and very active.

On the Heart

VITAMIN DEFICIENCIES AND HEART DISORDERS

Nutritional disorders may affect the heart as well as other organs, and sometimes seriously. Relief is not always obtain-

able by digitalis or diuretics, but can sometimes be obtained by the administration of antineuritic vitamin B, as in brewers' yeast. Vitamin C is effective in increasing the urinary output, and an adequate supply of vitamin C complex, including lemon and orange juice, has been suggested for patients with cardiac problems.

Lactic acid seems to poison the heart muscle in the absence of vitamin B₁ and prevents its functioning at full rate. Sometimes, when B₁ is given, the lactic acid can be disposed of and the heart is soon healing and able to function at its normal rate.

Many heart patients are advised to limit their food intake to reduce weight, but they often do this by wrongly limiting their protein intake for a time. This, combined with the effect resulting from eating refined and overcooked foods, may be responsible for the vast incidence of fatal heart disease.

Regarding vitamin E: "Apparently the therapeutic explanation for Vitamin E is that it increases oxygen to the heart and other muscles. It dissolves clots if they are fresh or bypasses sites of older clots or vascular blocking, thus increasing the circulation. Alpha-tocopherol is uniquely valuable in the treatment of coronary occlusion." (This was reported by W. E. Shute, E. V. Shute et al. in "Alpha-Tocopherol Vitamin E in Cardiovascular Disease," 1954.)

Lecithin has been found by many researchers to reduce the amount of cholesterol in the blood. In proper dosage, it dissolves the fatty plaques which may already be in the arteries. At least three tablespoons, taken daily for three to six months, have been known to bring levels to normal range.

Vitamin B₆ (pyridoxine) works together with essential fatty acids, vitamin E, and the B vitamins to improve a slow heart beat, a heart murmur, palpitations of the heart, or enlarged and nervous hearts, according to a report in the "Journal of Chronic Diseases" in 1955.

I was the victim of a severe heart attack, a coronary thrombosis. A friend of mine who had a similar attack about the same time—one seemingly as bad as mine—went to a Canadian doctor while I was attended by an American doctor. He was out of bed in a week; I was bedridden for four weeks. He was outside doing light work while I was still sitting in the house in an easy chair making a sissy of myself.

After being under my doctor's care for one year, he could not understand why I still had so much of the pain diagnosed as angina pectoris. He was of the opinion that I was really suffering from some disease of the nerves, so he sent me to a neurologist.

My physician had previously told me that if I was careful, I could live another ten years. I am a high-cholesterol producer. I do not recommend that others do what I did, but I quit taking the expensive medicine I had been taking to reduce the cholesterol (I have found out since this might have eventually been harmful). I went on a strict, low-fat diet. I started on vitamin E, which had been recommended by his doctor to my friend, and, additionally, took some B vitamins, including B_{12}; 25,000 units a day of A; 25,000 units of D once a week; and some C. I take wheat germ every day; I eat no pork; I add safflower oil to skim milk for necessary fat; I eat very little bread (and hope to give it up altogether some day), and lots of fruit and vegetables (mostly from my own garden). We freeze a lot of fresh-picked vegetables.

I try to be active, for I feel exercise is very important. Today I am active in about five different groups. People cannot understand where I get all of my energy from. I cut 1,500 square feet of grass with a walking power-mower, and the clippings go back into the garden—there's no weed killer on my grass. I collect and repair toys 365 days a year for unfortunate children, collect clothing and knickknacks for difforont groups. I put in nine to ten hours a day, sometimes more.

Right now I feel I am good for another ten years. My wife is convinced that I am on the right track. She never believed too much in vitamins or in watching what one eats. She always told me that I worked too hard and my neighbors keep telling me to take it easy. I tell them that this is what one does after he is dead. I could write a book on my experiences since having a heart attack, but perhaps I have written too much already. I am also very happy to see that some of our American doctors are waking up. Perhaps they can cut down the amount of deaths from heart attacks in this country.

I suffered a heart attack, not a severe one, but one that was powerful enough to put me in the hospital for several weeks. The laboratory tests that were initiated upon my entry there showed that my cholesterol was far above normal—a reading of between 150 and 300 is considered normal, and my reading was 328. Orders were given for me to cut down on cheese, butter, cream, and a long list of favorite foods. Also, a medication was prescribed to lower this level, but, following my hospitalization, the medication failed to budge the level. I told my doctor I felt that I could lower the cholesterol reading by going back to a food supplement that I had an idea about.

He told me to carry on. So, off to the health-food store I went, and there purchased a large bottle of 8 grain (about 500-milligram) lecithin capsules. You should have seen the surprise on my doctor's face when, after taking my blood test, he learned that my cholesterol had gone down to a good normal count of 140.

On Hemorrhoids

I have had many experiences and benefits from health information. I am now seventy-two years old and exercise a great deal of caution in using vitamins and minerals. I do take dolomite tablets [magnesium] for the treatment of hemorrhoids, but I must add that doing the following exercise also has something to do with controlling and reducing hemorrhoids. First draw in the buttocks and at the same time draw in the abdomen; hold for a count of seven, then let go. This exercise strengthens the muscles in the abdomen and prevents it from sagging, and it also acts as a restraining force on the hemorrhoids which causes the sacs to compress. I have been doing this exercise faithfully over the past six years, and now my hemorrhoids are almost at the vanishing point.

On Hydrochloric Acid

People over forty years of age begin to lose some of their normal hydrochloric acid because of a lack of the natural foods which stimulate this production.

Apple-cider vinegar is excellent to maintain the acid-alkaline balance so necessary for the body's assimilation of all nutrients. This balance can be checked daily by the use of Squibb's Nitrazine paper. A half-inch strip laid across the tongue on arising will show whether you are too acid or too alkaline.

There are hydrochloric acid tablets with pepsin if you prefer them to the cider vinegar.

Folk Medicine *by Dr. D. C. Jarvis (Holt, Rinehart*

and Winston) is a good book to read about the use of cider vinegar.

I had many aches and pains and felt sick after eating. My food was eliminated undigested. I was cold and short of breath after the mildest exertion. I also had a loss of hair, low blood pressure, and skin discoloration. After I had blood tests done and X rays taken, the doctor said, "You have low blood sugar and lack of calcium." He said there was something wrong in my digestive tract, and gave me some pills which didn't help.

I had been taking vitamins —A, B complex, and C—and minerals, but I had constant diarrhea. The doctor suggested I follow a bland diet, but that did not help me either. Then I read an article by a physician stating that people with my problem lacked digestive enzymes and hydrochloric acid, advising that hydrochloric acid be given by injection. I had my own physican communicate with this doctor and he did start me on the injections of hydrochloric acid.

I was also given pancreatic enzymes and bile salts, and my digestion improved. Once I improved, I stopped taking the injections and took the hydrochloric acid by mouth. Of course, I was put back on my much-needed vitamins and minerals as soon as I was able to digest them.

I had been looking for something to help me with my problem of gastritis. I knew I was lacking in hydrochloric acid, but could not find any information on how to obtain it.

In one of the health books a physician stated that applecider vinegar is a natural substitute for hydrochloric acid. He suggested taking two teaspoons of it mixed with two teaspoons of raw honey in a glass of hot water. I sip this slowly during meals three times a day. The honey and vinegar form an excellent combination of trace elements and vitamins which are needed to keep the body in good health. I feel I have benefited by following this suggestion and improving my diet.

On Hypoglycemia

Persons who suffer from hypoglycemia—an abnormal decrease of sugar in the blood—will find that proper dietary management is indispensable for getting well and staying well. Following are some nutritional suggestions for a high-protein, ample-fat, low-carbohydrate diet that includes a list of basic foods and suggestions for their use. A list of foods with hidden sugars is also included, as most of us are unaware of the enormous quantities of sugar present in foods and beverages.

For the obese or those concerned even with small increases of weight, every calorie must be counted, and it is best that they be taken in nutritious, wholesome, and tasty food.

Persons with low blood sugar or those who are constantly hungry will do better to eat smaller amounts at one sitting but eat more frequently, with meals broken down as suggested.

Note: You may have any fresh vegetable juice you desire. You may eat three baked white potatoes each week. You may eat liver as often as you wish. Avoid absolutely all desserts and beverages in which sugar is used, including pies, pastries, cookies, ice cream, soda fountain drinks and soda pop, candies, and the like.

HYPOGLYCEMIA DIET

On arising: An orange, half grapefruit, or 4 ounces of orange juice or grapefruit juice, or a combination of vegetable and fruit juices such as grape, apple, cranberry, or blended carrot and celery juice.

For breakfast: Choice of fruit or juice; 1 egg or some other part of the 8 ounces of protein allowed for the day; 1 slice of whole grain bread, if desired; herb tea or decaffeinated coffee with skim milk. *Note:* In your juice or cereal you can use Fay Lavan's Mix.°

Two Hours later: 4 ounces of tomato juice mixed with 1 teaspoon of Fay Lavan's Mix,° or 1 teaspoon desiccated liver† powder.

Lunch: Choice of meat, fish, or cheese; mixed salad of raw vegetables with cold-pressed oil dressing; fresh fruit, beverage.

Three hours after lunch: A snack of nuts with dried apricots or raisins.

Dinner: Same as lunch, but vary the proteins and use 4 to 6 ounces, with a salad and vegetables.

Prebedtime snack: Fruit juice or milk. *Note:* Prune juice, grapes, bananas, figs, and dates not only have a high calorie count but produce high carbohydrate grams and should be restricted, if you are watching your weight.

HIDDEN SUGARS

Specialists in nutrition and megavitamin therapy agree that the concentrated carbohydrate foods—soft drinks, candy, ice cream, pastries, and white-flour products—plus coffee and cigarettes are the factors most largely responsible for the widespread condition of hypoglycemia.

Statistics point up that an average of well over 100

°See the Index.

†It is best to mix desiccated liver in vegetable or tomato juice. Start with a very small amount until you become accustomed to the taste. Or blend with a little lemon juice.

pounds of sugar a year is consumed in America by every man, woman and child, as compared to only 10 pounds over the same period about a century ago, and there has been an equal increase in the populace in the degenerative diseases such as diabetes and arthritis, as well as an increase in the number of dental cavities, premature aging, fatigue, general aches and pains, and, of course, hypoglycemia.

It is estimated that more research is carried on in the United States than anywhere else in the world. Though this is commendable, something about which Americans can be proud, the findings stated in the paragraph above have not made enough impact to bring about the changes in the American diet necessary to slow this degeneration.

People who say, "I never eat sugar," might be surprised by the amount of sugar present in popular foods and drinks as noted in the table below:

SERVING	AMOUNT OF SUGAR
6 oz. cola	3½ teaspoons
8 oz. orangeade	5 teaspoons
8 oz. soda pop	5 teaspoons
1 cup sweet cider	6 teaspoons
10 oz. root beer	4½ teaspoons
3 oz. whiskey sour	½ teaspoon
4-oz. slice iced chocolate cake	10 teaspoons
4-oz. slice chocolate cake	6 teaspoons
1 chocolate eclair	7 teaspoons
4-oz. slice angel food cake	7 teaspoons
1 cupcake	6 teaspoons
1 glazed doughnut	6 teaspoons
1 macaroon	6 teaspoons
4-oz. slice fruitcake	5 teaspoons
4-oz. slice pound cake	5 teaspoons
1 fig newton	5 teaspoons
4 oz. hard candy	20 teaspoons
1 gumdrop	3½ oz.
1 oz. peanut brittle	3½ oz.
1 chocolate bar or chocolate cream or chocolate mint	2 or more teaspoons

My problem for many years has been one of constant hunger and a desire for sweets, which in turn led to my being overweight. I have now learned that we must not turn our backs and close our minds to suggestions of possible merit in nutrition. I know that I have now solved many of my problems by strict adherence to the principles of good nutrition.

I avoid absolutely all desserts and beverages in which sugar is used, such as pies, pastries, cookies, ice cream, fountain drinks, soda pop, and candies. I have also eliminated starchy foods such as spaghetti, macaroni, and noodles, and such beverages as wine, cordials, cocktails, and beer.

I eat frequent small meals to prevent blood-sugar starvation by keeping a trickle of usable sugars constantly going into my bloodstream. Fruit or fruit juices taken on arising start the body's machinery and a protein breakfast helps it work.

Protein is a daily necessity. Next to water, the body is made up chiefly of protein, and because the body does not store it, protein must be replaced daily. To make certain that I get my quota for the day I have 4 ounces of cottage cheese, fish, poultry, liver, or other meat for lunch and dinner. Each 4-ounce portion equals approximately 20 grams of protein. One egg is 8 grams and 2 glasses of milk or buttermilk are 16 grams.

For my afternoon snack I have 2 ounces of unsalted nuts mixed with a few raisins. I find protein tablets or high-protein powder very easy to take in between meals, in juice or soup.

Everyone planning a new health program will find that smaller meals prevent overeating. My idea that low blood sugar required sugar at these low periods was a great mistake. Nothing could be further from the truth, and yet this erroneous treatment for low blood sugar continues.

When lunchtime came around at summer camp, I always opened my crinkled brown bag to find a terribly unfashionable assortment of goodies.

Instead of packaged cookies, for instance, there would be carrots or celery sticks, and in place of cupcakes there would be assorted fruits. To top it off, my sandwich was always made of dark bread—extremely unsightly, in the eyes of my young contemporaries.

Throughout junior and senior high school my friends were continuously surprised by the unusual eating habits my mother was teaching me. I savored sunflower seeds and raisins while they munched candies, potato chips, and other snacks. Friends who came home for dinner never failed to exclaim at the strange color of the turbinado sugar. It seemed as if we always had "special" this or "healthier" that.

I must confess that I resented the fact that mom made me be "different," but as time went on I realized what she was teaching me. That was to use my common sense.

I found myself avoiding supermarket foods and turning instead toward the natural foods—luscious fruits and vegetables and unrefined products.

Trouble, however, arrived when I went away to college and found myself faced with the typical fare there: overcooked foods devoid of nutrients, and loads of soft drinks, sweets, and carbohydrates to fill me up.

I was under a great deal of tension, which caused me to crave even more of the only foods easily available to me. The tendency to run down to the "fat machines"—vending machines—on campus was in truth beginning to break down both my budget and my health. I began to tire very easily, and when winter came I found it almost impossible to stay warm. I suspected something was really wrong when I began getting headaches for no apparent reason and suffered spells of heavy heartbeats.

Following a series of tests, the doctor diagnosed my problem as hyperinsulinism. The name alone was enough to frighten me into clinging to the vitamin supplements he prescribed and doing my best to avoid sweets and carbohydrates.

I was soon able to turn my attention back to my education and to relax and once again enjoy living.

My mother taught me the value of natural, properly handled foods, reinforcing the fact that if you use God's gifts with common sense, they can bring you great happiness.

I am a working mother with two teenagers, a boy and a girl. I carry on a large dress-designing business.

My low period was four o'clock. Then I would feel completely exhausted and develop a migraine headache. It was suggested that I look to nutrition to change this, for with my schedule, I was not taking time to eat properly. The change I made benefited my children, my husband and myself. I began gradually, first fortifying the morning cereal with high-protein powder made of noninstant powdered milk, wheat germ, lecithin granules, and brewers' yeast, which I mixed together and stored in a large jar in the refrigerator. I soon added this mixture to meat loaf, hamburgers, or whatever food called for breading or other fillers. My family accepted this without too much fuss.

I also took several high-protein tablets with fruit, cheese, and a cup of herb tea at four o'clock in place of pastry or coffee. What a difference this change in eating habits made in only a short time! Even my clients complimented me on my newfound energy.

On Menopause

I had been seeking help to see me through the years of my approaching menopause. I was frightened at the prospect of taking hormones, as there is so much adverse information about their being the possible cause of breast cancer and blood clots.

Several of my friends have had breast cancer. Others have suffered severe torture, mental and physical, during and after menopause. Several others have taken natural estrogen hormones and they have been helped to some extent, but none of them had tried the nutritional approach to this problem.

I changed my diet to include such natural foods as wheat germ (which contains zinc), seafoods, kelp, brewers' yeast, peas, nuts, whole grains, watercress, spinach, kale, vitamins, and mineral supplements. Vitamin E and wheat-germ oil are also included in my diet.

Now my time has come and gone without any bad symptoms.

On Mental Depression and Illness

DRUGS VS. NUTRITION AND VITAMINS

There are many popular brand-name drugs on the market—potions and palliatives that are supposed to calm the nerves, cheer the depressed, rouse the drowsy, relieve the sleepless, and make the dull sparkle—the efficacy of which the government is challenging.

These drugs contain caffein, to wake you up and anti-histamines to cause drowsiness, and side effects have been reported for many. There is little clinical data on these over-the-counter drugs. The millions spent on promoting them through television and other advertising media influence people to believe that pills can change their moods and solve their problems. The manufacturers maintain that these drugs are safe when taken according to directions. But it would be better for the users to·get their "kicks" from nutrition.

Niacin, one of the B-complex vitamins (B_3), is now being used as a natural substitute for most of these over-the-counter drugs. The usual dose is 100 milligrams a day. Physicians are even using 3 to 10 grams daily for schizophrenia.

Dr. William Kaufman reported that there were additional benefits, such as gains in muscle strength, working capacity, decreased fatigability, an improved sense of equilibrium, and relief from certain emotional disorders, including depression from B_3.

The general medical profession is still reluctant to accept the theory that food is the major cause of many chronic illnesses today, and that proper nutrition and vitamin therapy could alleviate these conditions.

One of my sons had a "nervous breakdown" (diagnosed as schizophrenia) at the beginning of his senior year in college, although he had had psychological difficulties for many years prior to that, as well as mysterious physical complaints for which the medical profession found no cause. The first two psychiatrists we consulted did him no permanent good and some harm; the first one gave up on him altogether, saying my son had "decided" to become an invalid, while the second seemingly encouraged him to smoke and drink.

The turning point came somewhat over a year ago, when we found a psychiatrist who is also a nutritionist and who has adopted the biochemical approach to so-called mental disease. This doctor began a modified Hoffer and Osmond treatment, after first testing the "mauve factor" emphasized by Abram Hoffer and Humphry Osmond in *How to Live with Schizophrenia* (University Books). He also treated my son for hypoglycemia (using the six-hour glucose-tolerance test), and for a number of vitamin and mineral deficiencies. Our son is now on a hypoglycemia diet, gets megavitamin therapy, has a high intake of several other vitamins, and is given twice-monthly injections of adrenal-cortex extract, since he is also thought to have a malfunction of the adrenal-cortex gland. He required an awful lot of persuasion to agree to this regimen, needing to be shown as well as told that the diet and vitamins are essential. Therefore I went on the high-protein, low-carbohydrate diet myself, and began taking vitamin supplements designed for my own needs. Both of us have benefited tremendously.

It cannot be said that my son is cured, but he has definitely been kept out of the hospital twice in the past year. He seems improved in many areas, both psychological and physical, and seems to slip back only when he neglects—or refuses to follow—his regimen. His acne, nosebleeds, colds and sinus trouble, constipation, and nausea are all better or nonexistent. I shall always wonder whether, if he could have had megavitamin therapy ten years ago, he would ever have come to the point of considering himself "only half a human being."

My own benefits from improved (although admittedly not perfected) nutrition include relief from greatly swollen legs and spiderweb veins; gradual disappearance of many liver spots; longer hair (with some darkening of the gray); less fatigue; freedom from minor aches for which I formerly consumed considerable aspirin; relief from burning, gummy eyes; and better health of gums.

I have a son with schizophrenia. Today I sent along to our doctor an article entitled "New Help for the Schizophrenic," telling about the very effective reults obtained by giving these patients high dosages of vitamin B₃. I was very elated that the doctor responded in the affirmative and agreed with the article. As of today, thanks to the article, he has my son on this nicotinic-acid vitamin. This information, together with improved nutrition, has been a very great help.

I recently read an article on how schizophrenia is being treated with a high dosage of vitamin B₃ (niacin).

My sister-in-law has suffered from this illness since the birth of her children more than ten years ago. She has had electric shock and insulin treatment, but to no avail.

I sent the article on to my brother with the hope that they might try this new approach. My sister-in-law was readmitted to the hospital for vitamin treatment with niacin and a complete nutritional program, including small, frequent meals with all the vitamin and mineral supplements.

In his last letter to me my brother stated that his wife is enjoying newfound health and is able to participate in all family affairs.

My problem was chronic depression. I wondered what it would really be like to feel young, vibrant, and healthy. Now I know it need no longer be a dream. It can be a reality for you and your family as it has been for me.

The answer is throw out the carbohydrates. In their place use honey, molasses, and fresh fruits. The second step is to change to whole grains in place of white pap. Learn to use wheat germ (and to enjoy its wonderful qualities), brewers' yeast for the B vitamins, lecithin for lowering cholesterol, and desiccated liver powder in vegetable and tomato juices.

One of the added benefits received from using newfound nutritional knowledge is lower doctor's bills—and all of these benefits came about in a few short months.

On Nutrition

VOLUNTEERS FOR BETTER NUTRITION

Dr. Edwin L. Crosby of the American Hospital in Paris states: "This year one out of every seven Americans will use a hospital, and 50 percent will use it for outpatient nonacute services. We must now be concerned with keeping people out of the hospitals—with the preventive, the curative, and the rehabilitative aspects of illness." Many of these patients could be helped materially through nutrition—by being taught new eating patterns.

Today, two-thirds of our nonprofit community hospitals are served by volunteers. Almost 90 percent of these volunteers are women. Along with the many other services they perform, these volunteers could direct a program to introduce the patients to new ways to prepare fresh fruits, vegetables, and salads (perhaps farmers from nearby areas could be induced to contribute some fresh produce) in place of the canned foods so many of them use; they could teach the patients to choose fruit drinks in place of soda or coffee for between-meal beverages; and introduce them to whole grain bread, possibly made at home by some of these same volunteers (that would be a real contribution!). One other food to which the patients should be introduced is a healthful cereal consisting of wheat germ, lecithin, high-protein powder, and brewers' yeast,* served with sliced bananas (to

---

*See Fay Lavan's Mix in the Index.

supply extra potassium) and reconstituted powdered skim milk, the whole making an excellent substitute for nonnutritious corn flakes or other commerical—and generally sugared —cereals.

SEXUAL PROBLEMS

Dr. Willard Dalrymple (no relation), director of health services at Princeton University, was reported in a recent newspaper article to have stated that the most frequent problem, after colds, of male Princetonians, is concern over sexual inadequacy. Likewise, at Stanford University, Dr. James McClenahan, director of health, has reported that the common cold, flu, and other viral diseases constitute the most frequent illnesses among the undergraduates, and that those men who seek sexual advice are most concerned with their impctency. He concedes that drugs and liquor also figure as problems, but not to the same extent.

Dr. Paavo Airola, in his book Sex and Nutrition, *states that all endocrine glands can work at their full potential only if the body is given proper nourishment. Vitamin E is vitally important for the sexuality of both men and women, and Dr. Airola states that testosterone (the male hormone) and estrogen (the female hormone) are equally important for a good sex life and general health, and that their lack can cause mental depression and unexplained unhappiness.*

Other specific vitamins than can aid in this area are all the Bs—B$_1$, B$_2$, B$_3$, B$_6$ and—vitamin F (essential fatty acid, at least 2 tablespoons a day, taken as vegetable oil). Also good are pumpkin seeds, and kelp (for iodine and the thyroid function). The charts in Part Three provide additional helpful information.

I have been looking for an answer to my unexplained health

problems. My physical checkup showed no abnormalities, yet I complained of aches, pains, depression, and fatigue, none of which seemed to have a logical explanation. I was told I would simply have to "live with it." I was never asked what foods I ate.

I believed I was getting an adequate protein diet. I had one egg a day; a hamburger or sandwich with coffee or Coke for lunch; meat, potato and another vegetable, and pie for dessert at dinner; and I considered this nourishing. I did not know about hidden sugars in the food I was eating, or what they were doing to the vitamin B, undersupplied to start with, in my body. I did not know that foods containing vitamins and protein had to be supplied to the body each day, as they are not stored by the body. I did not know that healthful eating could be a pleasant and exciting adventure once I learned its secrets.

I found the answer to my health problems by reading health magazines and books on vitamins and minerals in foods. I learned how to enrich my own recipes, and the simple changes in my everyday routine brought extra energy, self-confidence, poise and proper weight—all this by a few changes in my eating habits. I would rather pay food bills than doctor bills. Though not a health nut, I'm nuts about being healthy.

Did you know that some of the biggest stars of ballet are in their forties? Even fifties? I am, yet my body remains youthfully trim and graceful, and I'm able to burn up a vast amount of energy without tiring. How do I do it? Well, rigorous exercise is a normal part of my work. But more than that, I rely on natural foods and vitamin supplements to maintain my youthful vigor and muscle tone, to keep my body sound, healthy, and at the peak of physical perfection.

Vitamin C and vitamin E are special favorites of "middle-aged" performers who display limitless energy and youthful form despite tremendous physical strain. Seeds, honey, fresh vegetables, juices, wheat germ—all are familiar parts of my diet. Next time you feel inclined to shout "Bravo!" at a ballet, reserve some of your cheers for Mother Nature.

The most amazing things have happened to me. I never dreamed what just changing our eating habits could mean. I was resigned to always being tired, to having tooth cavities, tartar on my teeth, brown spots on my hands, pimples on my muddy-colored face, pus in my ears, bleeding gums, oily hair and face, itching dandruff, arthritis in my hands. Now I know that no one needs to have these things.

No longer do my eyes twitch or water, and my eyesight has improved. My drab hair is once again a bright blonde. Many people now comment on my clear skin. I sleep all night—which still surprises me. But I do get my exercise! I raise enough of a garden organically to feed us all year, mow an acre of lawn each week, care for my flower beds, all the animals, and our continuous company. All this—and never once think of being tired.

Now, at sixty-seven, it is a joy to work all day without a pain or ache.

I have to stay slim and trim because I am a professional model.

I used to go on a very strict (nonnutritional) diet. Usually the results were quick, but I always looked tired, with deep circles around the eyes. Of course, being a model, I could hide the circles with makeup.

Since then, I have changed my eating habits and have been getting the proper vitamins and minerals, and I feel 100 percent better. I must look better, too, for I have been getting more modeling assignments!

Like many other mothers, I am faced with the problem of what to do about the cafeteria food served at the school my three sons will attend. Fortunately, it is only lunch. Since school opened, the older boy (seven) has been taking his lunch with him. This consists of a sandwich—homemade whole grain bread with a nourishing filling—carrot sticks, and an apple or variations of this.

A few days ago he came home and asked: "Why am I the only boy who has dark bread for my sandwich and no candy or cookies?" My reply was: "How many children have been out of school with colds and sickness this term?" He answered, "All of them except me." I then explained again the ill effects of "junk foods," the lack of nourishment in white bread, and that other mothers had not yet learned the difference between that and our bread—although I hoped that they too would someday understand the difference—or were too busy to bake bread.

I decided to make some peanut butter and honey cookies so that he would not feel too different, and I gave him a choice between white bread (made of unbleached flour, of course), or dark, but he chose to continue with his dark bread. This, of course, pleased me very much.

I am trying to instill good nutrition habits in my three little boys, explaining to them the differences between honey and sugar, white and dark bread, our lollipops (which I make from fresh orange juice and put on a stick, place in the freezer and serve in place of ice cream), and the commercial kind.

We have peanut butter cookies, brownies made with carob and sesame, and honey balls in place of candy.

I am fortunate that my husband takes an interest in our new way of eating and each morning joins me in our special drink, which includes brewers' yeast, wheat germ, lecithin, and high-protein powder.

The children love raw vegetables as well as those I prepare in a steamer. They accompany me to the health-food store as well as the supermarket and help me select our foods and read the labels. They eat "junk foods" only at parties where I cannot control the menu, but I often hear them say to their friends, "Mommy doesn't like us to eat that." If you can inculcate them young with the importance of health, even teen-agers can be made aware of what is happening around them. After all, they are now ecology conscious and they can also be made food conscious.

There is much to be done. With an alert citizenry, perhaps school lunchrooms can be improved. For instance, mothers could help prepare fresh foods instead of canned vegetables, but this will take time and I will wait patiently for that day to come.

Though I have been interested in good nutrition—or what I considered good nutrition—for many years, I had my eyes really opened as to how inadequate my nutrition had been after a visit to a health-food store two years ago.

I went there for the purpose of buying pumpkin seeds to cure tapeworm in my dog. I had read in a book by an old country doctor that this treatment could possibly eliminate this parasite. It did! For about six weeks, I ground up the seeds and added a tablespoon or so to my dog's diet daily. And he enjoyed the extra goodie, too!

That was only the beginning. The sincerity of the intelligent owner of the store piqued my interest further in nutrition by discussing the merits of certain vitamins, etc., and she suggested I read books on nutrition.

The result was a list of benefits that I would never had believed possible. With vitamins A and E, my skin texture improved immensely. Since taking vitamin E I've not experienced hot flashes, though I had both ovaries removed. I can walk up a steep hill from our lake shore with no labored breathing. Swimming is easy now; I get no feeling of breathlessness. I have no more leg cramps (thanks to E and calcium); because of C, I have had no colds for two years. Bruising, bleeding gums, and hemorhoids are controlled by C and B₆ particularly.

The best bonus of all, one that still amazes me, was to be able to ride horseback without the heavy Camp corset I had been wearing for ten years due to a degenerated disc in my back. Doctors told me when I had that first distressing episode of not being able to straighten up after bending over that I shouldn't ride at all. Well, that was too hard to swallow, so with special exercises to strengthen supporting muscles and vitamin B₁₂ injections once a week, plus 1 tablespoon of cod liver oil taken three or four times a week, I was able to ride in moderation. Cantering was impossible, though, and trotting (on a Cadillac of a horse) was kept to a minimum.

Since I've taken daily 25,000 units of vitamin A, 2 vitamin B-complex tablets, 2,000 milligrams of C, calcium (with D included) with magnesium, 600 units of E (started with 1,200 units), minerals, 3 tablespoons lecithin, and yeast, I've become flexible again. Now my horseback riding includes lengthy trotting sessions, and cantering is a joy once more.

Of course, not everyone should take the same amounts of vitamins. One has to determine her own needs, and even these will change from time to time.

Now I'm interested in purchasing a juicer. Maybe there will be some new surprises to make this middle-aged body even more buoyant.

On the Prostate

For the past few years I have had prostate trouble. I visited one of the best urologists in my area. He found I had an infection in both the prostate and the bladder, so he gave me a prescription to cure it. But I did not have it filled, for a friend told me he had read in medical journals that the medics said that cranberry juice did more for infections than their drugs, so I began drinking 6 ounces of cranberry juice three times a day.

A week later I kept a date to return to the urologist. He said the infection was cleared up in the bladder but I still had some infection in the prostate. A week later I kept another appointment I had with him. I had continued drinking cranberry juice, and on this examination he said the infection was cleared up in both the prostate and the bladder.

We grow organic produce and do believe that the food today that has been commercially fertilized and chemically treated is probably the number one reason hospitals are kept full. I do not use drugs or medicine in any way. I eat organic vegetables and foods and take organic vitamins only.

Five years ago my husband had a prostate infection. He saw a urologist who prescribed an antibiotic. The infection cleared up, but he was to have to be checked periodically.

There are several books available about the treatment of prostate difficulties by nutrition. These suggested pumpkin seeds, which I ground and put into breakfast cereal into which I also mixed wheat germ. Essential fatty acid was suggested, and I managed to get two tablespoons into salad dressing each day in the form of safflower oil.

At each successive visit the doctor proclaimed the condition no worse, and this continued for five years. The frequency of urination both day and night and some difficulty in retention and the possibility of infection finally made an operation advisable.

My husband is a professional man and not one to make fast judgments, so he had me do some research first. We found that there were two types of surgery: open, and transurethral prostatectomy (closed surgery). The open method takes less time in surgery, requires a hospital stay of one week to ten days, and two to three weeks recuperation. The closed surgery takes one hour and requires a hospital stay of three to five days, with recovery depending on one's physical condition. The hospital, on taking my husband's history, could not believe, from his reactions, tests, etc., that he was in his early seventies. On the fourth day, when he was ready to leave the hospital, the nurses asked him his secrets and he referred them to me. He resumed his office work a week later, and has been enjoying excellent health since then.

What do we do? It is simple. We eat wisely and simply. Our meals are planned to give us each our quota of protein, with emphasis on B complex from brewers' yeast and wheat germ, fresh fruits and vegetables for vitamin C as well as C with bioflavonoids, calcium from bone meal, calcium lactate, vitamins A, D, and E, and a good all-purpose vitamin for the minerals and the amino acids.

We hope this may help someone who has to make a decision about a prostate operation.

On Reducing

Just about everyone fights overweight at one time or another. Mine is the five- to ten-pound problem. These unwanted pounds usually accumulate during holiday trips or weekends, due to carbohydrate snacking. My dresses begin to feel tight, and this is a better indicator than the scale.

Since it is crucial for everyone to keep his weight down (for cholesterol goes up for each pound of added weight), some medics consider a gain of three pounds a more serious thing than if your thermometer showed three degrees above normal in temperature. Attaining and maintaining an ideal weight is most important.

But fasting and excessive dieting with too little carbohydrate intake may bring on unusual pain across the back, under the shoulder blades. Sometimes it raises uric acid levels, causing gout pains in the toes. These pains are caused by a depletion of pantothenic acid and vitamin C, and these and other balanced vitamins, such as B complex and E, should be taken when dieting.

Keeping a chart, a scale, and a tape measure, and weighing oneself at the same time each day, helps to keep one aware of changes in weight. Too much fruit juice and raw fruit in the same day without enough protein and fat will start the cycle of weight increase.

In order to feel really well, I must have the proper amount of food and supplements. Any deviation brings on strange aches and pains. I finally settled for wearing a larger dress size. Instead of starving myself to be a size 10, I am now a happy and comfortable 12.

For me, frequent and small meals are the answer. I eat cereal with wheat germ, brewers' yeast, lecithin, and high-protein powder with skim milk for breakfast. Several hours later I have 1 boiled egg, a ½ slice of whole grain bread, cottage cheese, 1 piece of fruit, and buttermilk or yogurt. My afternoon snack is nuts and raisins, and for dinner I have some kind of protein with salad and vegetables.

I have found that eternal vigilance is the price of keep ing slim, and weight reduction must be done gradually, if one is to avoid side effects.

I am now happy and comfortable in my size 12, and for one in the mid-sixties who feels like thirty, that is not too bad.

I was shocked to learn that I had developed some problems by age sixty-six that I had hoped to avoid. My blood pres- sure had always been normal or low, and now it was ele- vated—not alarmingly, but unaccountably. My uric acid was high, and I had a few toe twinges at night. My albumin was low.

Where had I gone wrong? The doctor who did the tests was uncertain what had brought this about, and so I turned to nutritional literature. I recalled that on a recent trip abroad I found the meat in restaurants unpalatable and had not had meat for nearly three weeks, even though I did have other protein. I did not have my full supply of vitamin-rich foods nor as many supplements as I was accustomed to take, and yet I had gained weight on the trip due to exces- sive snacking on sweets. On my return home I started on a restricted diet to try to lose this excess weight.

Since my blood showed low albumin, the doctor told me to increase my protein. He explained that when the diet is low in protein, sufficient albumin cannot be formed, and waste materials are not completely removed from the tissues. I immediately remedied this by checking my protein at each meal. To my breakfast cereal I added 2 tablespoons of wheat germ, 3 tablespoons lecithin, 1 tablespoon brewers' yeast, and 1 tablespoon of a mixture of ground sesame, pumpkin seeds, sunflower seeds, and high-protein powder that I kept on hand for various uses, as well as half a banana and skim milk. I took my vitamins with vegetable juice, 1 egg and 1 slice whole grain bread. At 11:00 a.m. 1 had 4 ounces of cottage cheese.

For luncheon, at 1:00 p.m., 1 had 4 ounces of fish, and salad, and at 4:00 p.m., a snack of 2 ounces of nuts and raisins. At 7:00 p.m. I had fresh vegetable soup, 4 ounces protein (either meat or fish), and a fruit dessert. This was a total of approximately 60 or 70 grams for the day.

The doctor had also said that my slightly elevated uric acid was caused by a lack of protein, and could be helped by taking pantothenic acid added to vitamin E and to B₆ with magnesium oxide. I also added to my supplements 1 teaspoon concentrated cherry juice and ¼ to ½ pound of Bing cherries in season, as they too are recommended for gout.

On Skin Problems

Millions of dollars are spent on glamorizing the "C" foods: colas, coffee, cigarettes, candy, chocolate, creams, cookies, cakes, chips, commercial cereals, chewing gum, canned goods and crackers. No wonder some children and teen-agers think these are the only foods that merit attention! Yet overindulgence can result in boils, pimples, acne, and other skin eruptions as the body attempts to rid itself of the toxins caused by these food indiscretions.

One of the physicians who attended the White House Conference on Food, Nutrition, and Health, recently said: "There is profound ignorance of scientific nutrition at all levels of our society, from Pentagon officials down to the poorest

people. *The widespread and severe malnutrition which
exists in our society and throughout the world is not emo-
tionally perceived by any significant number of our citizens;
even those who profess interest in nutrition and malnutrition
do not really understand the role that malnutrition has in
causing so much preventable disease and death among our
people at all age levels and in all socio-economic strata. The
role of the private food, soft drink, snack, and cigarette industries in maintaining the malnutrition of our people is not
clearly perceived. This is why the White House Conference
failed to identify the major problems, the real reasons the
health and nutrition of the U.S. people continues to get
worse in the face of our agricultural abundance."*

Millions are spent on television and every other type of
advertising to promote empty-calorie foods. Have you ever
seen a TV commercial for fresh-squeezed fruit drinks, carob
(St. John's Bread) to replace chocolate; for nuts and raisins
as snacks in place of potato chips; for wheat germ; for brewers' yeast; for lecithin granules as a cereal or addition to
other cereals (to raise the vitamin B level and replace
vitamins and minerals that have been removed by the pro-
cessing methods now in use)? These foods are advertised
only in health-oriented magazines and reach a limited audi-
ence, who are already familiar with their virtues.

Dermatologists are aware that a vitamin E deficiency is
responsible for many of the more serious skin problems.

*"The original association of vitamin E with fertility has
tended to distract attention from its wide range of physiological activity, and to many it is still regarded simply as the
'fertility vitamin.' Actually, vitamin E is intimately involved
in many physiological functions at the intracellular level of
probably all tissues of the body, so that its deprivation, mal-
absorption, or regional malfunction is capable of producing
a great variety of clinical manifestations."* So said Samuel

Ayres, Jr., and Richard Mihan (both M.D.'s) in March 1969 in "*Cutaneous Medicine for the Practitioner,*" Vol. 5, No. 3, (Los Angeles).

Why was I not taught in school that acne is caused by a poor diet? Young people, particularly those with acne, should be told that all rich and overprocessed foods, especially carbohydrates, must be eliminated from their diet.

When I was given such a list of foods, including soda pop, candy, and ice cream, and told to eliminate them from my diet, I asked my doctor, "What else is there?" But, much to my amazement, I found there were many delicious, nutritious, and wholesome substitutes.

I was horrified to learn what overprocessing does to the nutritive value of foods. And what we do to food when we prepare it at home is unbelievable. For instance, I learned that by boiling potatoes, carrots, cabbage, and apples, we lose from 48 percent to 50 percent of their iron, calcium, phosphorous, and magnesium. I decided to eat more of my food raw, and I suggested to my mother that she use a steamer to cook vegetables so as to retain as much of the vitamins as possible.

My doctor did stress the importance of proper nutrition. Unfortunately, he did not go into detail. He said only, "Eat a well-balanced diet." I soon realized I would have much to learn.

I tried to find poison-free foods grown on fertile soil and to eat them fresh and not overcooked. Unfortunately, the price of organically grown food is too high for most people. However, if you are concerned about chemicals on fruits and vegetables, place them in a pan of water, sufficient to cover, in which you have put 1 teaspoon of basil, and let soak for 15 minutes.

Every day, while doing my homework, I eat two raw carrots (with the skin on, for vitamin A is contained near the skin). I chew these thoroughly.

My new diet has not only helped to clear up my acne but it has also given me unexpected dividends in improved stamina, better concentration, and a new feeling of well-being.

I was one among ten dermatology patients who had been classified as hopeless incurables and were used for diet studies. We were taken off all medication and placed on a low-carbohydrate-high-protein supplemental diet. Within two or four weeks our lesions were cured. We were given no follow-up instructions and most of us returned to our former diets. After four weeks I returned to the clinic for a checkup, and except for me, the lesions in our group had reoccurred.

I had realized that the improved diet had not only helped my skin problems, but it made me feel better and more alert. I had not gone back on the old diet in order to prove the study; I had enough proof in the way I felt.

I decided that following the diet was the only way to stay well. I kept a record of my food intake. I averaged 8 ounces of protein a day—4 ounces of fish or liver at lunch, and 4 ounces of poultry or meat at dinner. I ate 2 raw carrots a day, as well as cottage cheese or juice for vitamin A. I got vitamin E in wheat-germ oil and alpha-tocopherol capsules; I ate fresh fruit and vegetables, whole grains, and nuts and seeds in moderation.

I am happy I took part in this study. Through it, I learned that improper diet is not only the main cause of skin problems among teen-agers, but the cause of many chronic illnesses which nutrition and vitamins could help.

My husband is not one to take pills or vitamins, but I persuaded him to take vitamin E for general health and he consented. He had suffered from psoriasis in the most annoying places for forty years. At times it was quite bad.

At any rate, after about two weeks on 100 international units of vitamin E, the psoriasis seemed to be improved. It was certainly less itchy. We raised the intake to 400 units and the itch not only stopped completely but the scabs disappeared.

I have had a number of people tell me that when their physicians had put them on vitamin E for circulation or other problems, it also improved their psoriasis, if they had it.

My husband who had had psoriasis and had been taking E, ran out of it, and in four days the scabs returned. So it is apparent this vitamin must be continued if one is to be free of the problem. He wouldn't neglect taking it now for anything.

I feel this is marvelous as this nasty disease has never had much help from medicine.

On the Teeth

At age seventy, I still had a few of my own teeth left to which were attached bridges. I was fortunate to be able to avoid dentures. Then the dentist found that the remaining teeth on the bottom were getting loose due to gum erosion and suggested putting a brace on them to hold them in place. I agreed.

My wife was certain that this would not have happened if I was getting enough calcium and cut down on sweets. Since the dentist warned that if I did not retain these teeth I would indeed be in trouble, I gave up the sweets—I used to keep something sweet in my mouth all the time—for nuts and raisins, added bone-meal tablets to my vitamins, and high-protein powder to my cereal. Within one year the teeth had become stable and the dentist was able to remove the brace. It is now three years since I have had any trouble.

It must be true that nutrition helps the teeth. It certainly did in my case.

I had always had bad teeth; I usually went to the dentist every six months, and each time I had at least three or four cavities. The last time I went, there had been a hiatus of thirteen months between visits. But, wonder of wonders! I had only two very small cavities! And this after thirteen months, whereas it had not been unusual for me to have double that number in only six months! This drastic a change could only be attributed to my change in eating habits and the taking of vitamins and mineral supplements.

I am twenty years old and have been eating health foods and taking natural supplements for approximately two years. I take dolomite supplements—approximately two tablets a day (more, when I anticipate circumstances that will make me nervous); I drink lots of milk; and I've stopped eating sugar (no sodas, cakes, cookies, candies, or anything that contains refined white sugar; the only sugar I get is from fruits, fruit juices and honey).

More than fifty years ago, as a young girl, I was in bed for weeks with an undiagnosed pain in the side. Appendicitis was ruled out and I was given every type of cathartic, but nothing helped. Then, in a magazine, I read that infected teeth could cause pain in different parts of the body that was sometimes diagnosed as arthritis. I suggested to mother that I see our dentist. X rays showed three infected teeth. They were removed, and within a few days the pain was gone.

A few years later it became fashionable to blame the teeth for almost all body pain. Many dentists did unnecessary extractions, and dentures and removable bridgework were having their day. Needless to say, no one mentioned that good nutrition or the elimination of excessive carbohydrates might be a simple cure. Even natural carbohydrates such as raw sugar, honey, and dried fruits, when taken in excess, will affect the teeth and gums unless they are immediately cleansed.

I started to take calcium lactate and calcium glucomate in place of bone meal. I added glutamic acid and hydrochloric acid tablets, and a full supply of vitamins and minerals. This not only prevented further cavities but gave me more pep and zest.

On the Thyroid

My history was a constant round of hospitals—in and out—for thyroid, gallbladder, vague aches and pains, and you-name-it. I refused to submit to operations as I was never convinced of the need for them. I instinctively knew something was lacking in my system; it wasn't that something should be removed. If only I knew what to do to help myself! Health articles suggesting vitamins, minerals, and health foods did not receive wide praise from doctors and medical groups, and my husband insisted I follow their advice. Undaunted, I proceeded to look for an answer, and when I found it, I could not believe it was so simple.

I started with vitamins A and D, 25,000 units; B_1 and B_2, 25 units; B_3, 50 units; C, 1,000 to 3,000 depending on whether I had an oncoming cold; vitamin E, 400 units for improved circulation and avoiding leg cramps; vitamin B_6 to reduce edema (water retention); and kelp tablets for iodine (for my thyroid).

To my cereal I added wheat germ, brewers' yeast (and

worked up from a teaspoon to 3 tablespoons daily), and three tablespoons of lecithin granules. This brought my cholesterol down to normal.

I am not suggesting this is a panacea, but by applying these measures, I have helped myself.

My daughter was born with a goiter because of a malfunctioning thyroid gland. When she reached the age of five, it was so bad that I made an appointment with my family physician and a good surgeon to discuss it. Both doctors gave me the same diagnosis: the goiter would have to be removed. The surgeon told me to watch it very closely and if there was any surge of growth to let him know immediately.

My aunt and uncle, who had just opened up a health-food store, had been studying nutrition for many years. They advised me to start giving my daughter comfrey and kelp tablets and garlic perles daily. She had always had a more than adequate diet. I took their advice.

Within a year after I began my daughter's corrective regimen, all the swelling around her neck disappeared. I waited another year, then took her back to the surgeon. He was amazed to find the goiter gone. She is now twelve years old and has no sign of a goiter.

On Vitamin E

Some people ask, "Why do we need vitamin E?" The answer is: Because we do not get it from our overprocessed foods. As our food goes through many channels before it reaches our tables, much if not all of the vitamin E is destroyed by storage and overcooking.

Vitamin E was discovered over fifty years ago. It was first accepted for use in animal nutrition. In 1959 the FDA ap-

proved it as a necessary element in human nutrition. There are, however, many physicians who still refuse to recognize its wonderful healing powers.

The role of vitamin E in the prevention and treatment of diseases has not yet fully been explored, but it seems evident that it has played a part in helping psoriasis, the skin ailment for which little has been done by medicine. There is continuing research on vitamin E for skin problems and for peptic ulcer. Also, it has helped leg cramps, asthma, deep wounds, burns, phlebitis, and warts. It is prescribed in cases of infertility. It is even used in treatment of heart problems (the work of the Drs. Shute in Canada in this for over twenty-five years is well known and documented). Apparently, vitamin E increases oxygen to the heart and other muscles. It also, according to the Drs. Shute, dissolves clots if they are fresh, or helps the blood to bypass sites of older clots or vascular blocking.

Vitamin E is a fat-soluble vitamin that is derived from wheat-germ oil and is nontoxic. It has been suggested by a number of researchers that it should be taken with some fat, and the use of polyunsaturated fats increases the need for vitamin E. The use of vitamin E in combination with other vitamins and an improved nutritional program improves the body's efficiency and vitality.

There are several different forms of vitamin E. It is important to obtain the vitamin E with active alpha-tocopherol.

There are more than straws in the wind in the air-pollution problem, despite the assurances of the air-pollution control agencies. I am one of the cases now on record of people who are very sensitive to smog. I spend a great many hours in my car, and complained of nausea, headache, lethargy, and difficulty in staying awake at the wheel. The Tuberculosis Association of New York, quoted in a medical report I recently read, made me look to my nutrition and supplements to see if they could keep me well:

"Vitamins to Counteract Smog? Fat antoxidants such as vitamin E in the diet may offer some protection against respiratory diseases caused by air pollution. Laboratory tests with rats indicate 'that vitamin E is beneficial in protecting the lungs from obstructive lung diseases such as emphysema and edema that are caused by smog.' However, vitamin-E-supplemented diets will not cure already diseased lungs and it appears that it will offer protection only to certain levels of ozone or nitrogen dioxide concentrations."

The investigators found that rats given diets fortified with vitamin E lived twice as long as rats with an unfortified diet in an atmosphere simulating air-pollution concentrations like those found in Los Angeles or Tokyo on a bad day.

You can be tested for carbon monoxide in the blood if you are concerned with this problem. A level of 3 percent or over causes these adverse effects. Unless vitamin E intake is adequate, any vitamin A reaching the blood is destroyed and any already stored is quickly used up.

Eating rancid fats can induce further serious vitamin deficiencies. Vitamin E is quickly destroyed by rancidity. It should not be bought in too large a quantity; it should be of the highest quality, and kept cool and dark and dry.

The Department of Agriculture researchers have reported liver function aided by vitamin E, for it keeps sodium and potassium in balance. To sum up all the information I have researched, I found it shocking that many physicians refuse to recognize the benefits of vitamin E in nutrition. The following is typical of a reply in a physician's syndicated column; insult is added to injury when a question and answer such as the following appears:

QUESTION: Would you please tell me what vitamin E is and what it is good for? R.G.B.

ANSWER: Vitamin E has been under intense study for more than 25 years. It has been ascribed every magical benefit ever since it was first identified in 1922. If one were to believe in all its supposedly beneficial effects, we would all be free of almost every serious disease. In truth then, in spite of all of this investigation, there is no evidence that vitamin E is required at all in the diet of man. If you were a rabbit or a guinea pig you might need vitamin E, but as a member of Homo sapiens it is probably useless.

"We know a lot about diseases, but don't seem to pay enough attention to health," says Dr. Paul Dudley White.

I am at the ripe age of sixty, and just lately I've had such a terrible breakout on the skin under my breasts. I've had prescriptions for antibiotics and I've used everything anyone recommended. I am a user of vitamin E for my heart. One day I read of someone using vitamin E for an open sore. So while taking vitamin E one night I opened the capsules, and after washing off the sores, I put vitamin E on them. After doing this for three nights, to my great surprise the sores were completely healed. I want people to know of the miraculous vitamin E.

A member of my family had red welts on her arms from broken veins. Some even bled. The doctor said it was from old age and nothing could be done. I persuaded her to take 600 to 800 I.U.s of vitamin E daily and the condition cleared rapidly.

After my father-in-law suffered a heart attack, he read

about vitamin E in a book and asked the doctor about it. The doctor said he took vitamin E himself but didn't prescribe it for his patients.

Vitamins, I think, are slowly coming into their own. People are slowly learning, the hard way, just how important they are, just as my husband and I learned about vitamin E.

Several years ago my husband had rheumatism so badly in his left leg that he had to lift that leg in with his hands when getting into or out of the car. And he limped and dragged that leg when he walked, it was so painful. An old man who lived in back of us saw my husband limping around one day and came over. He told him that he had been the same way, then he started taking vitamin E. Now he was active and spry as could be. That did it.

My husband bought a big bottle of vitamin E. In a month's time he was walking as well as ever, and still is; that was almost six years ago. (Incidentally, he stills takes E faithfully.) At about the same time we heard how beneficial it is for heart trouble. I myself was up and down with a bad heart. I began taking vitamin E; still am. I hardly ever have pressure and chest pains any more. My health is so much better. Recently I purchased some dolomite, brewers' yeast, vitamins A and D.

Why do doctors laugh at vitamins? (And yet they are so quick to prescribe synthetic drugs.)

My granddaughter was bitten by a very vicious German shepherd on her cheek to within a half inch of her eye. We had a wonderful surgeon take care of the cheek and he told us to bring her back in three days.

I made my son apply the oil from 400 I.U. caps of vitamin E. Upon her return, the surgeon was astonished at the improvement and wanted to know how we did it. When we told him about vitamin E, he said he was going to recommend it to all his patients.

I will be eternally grateful to the Dr. Shute brothers. I have suffered two strokes and take 800 I.U. of vitamin E daily and never felt better.

My daughter, Margaret, is ten years old and on the swimming team. Every year she develops an infection commonly called swimmer's itch, caused by schistosomes (tiny worms) in the water.

After reading about the wonder vitamin E and its healing effects, I put vitamin E in the infected ear and each time I did so, it would be healed the next day. If it was badly infected, it would take two to three days to heal. The earlier you put the vitamin E in the ear, I believe, the faster the cure. It has worked for me and my daughter.

About two months ago my husband was in the cellar moving some sacks of onions, and a centipede bit him. I couldn't think of a thing to put on it except vitamin E. By that time the bite was swollen and very red. He put the vitamin on it several times and by the next morning it was OK.

I never use anything but vitamin E for burns, stings, and insect bites. It even stops the itching from mosquito bites. Sure would hate to be without vitamin E.

For nearly four years, I have had a seed wart and didn't know it. I asked a number of doctors what the strange growth was on the side of my thumb, but they called it a "weird fungus."

I had used a commercial wart remover for about two weeks several years ago, but it did nothing and I gave it up.

We have been getting organic vitamins, and the idea occurred to me to try vitamin E. I placed the vitamin E on a Band-Aid and applied it every night and morning, and after a few days it killed the root and the wart was gone and there was no pain.

When the roots finally gave way, they came off in a crusty patch with no bleeding. Under the scab was my thumb. I hadn't seen it in four years. Was I happy!

I am still treating my thumb with the E. I want to be very sure I have no scar and that my wart does not return.

Part Two

COOKING FOR HEALTH

Nutritional Therapy

It is encouraging to see that attitudes toward nutrition and vitamin therapy are gradually changing. Until very recently, people were labeled "faddists" and "cranks" if they suggested that vitamin C was helpful in preventing the common cold, that the oil from a vitamin E capsule would deaden the pain of minor burns and scraped knees, that the use of lecithin in the diet would reduce cholesterol, that sufficient protein should be eaten at every meal in order to rebuild the body cells, that too much white sugar and refined white flour were enemies of the human system, that fruit and fresh vegetables should be taken in place of irritating laxatives. Yet today, these and so many other theories like them are accepted, and it is now acknowledged that optimal growth, development, functions, and health require optimal nutrition. This we must obtain from products nourished by the soil and the sea. The quality of the soil in which our food is grown should be not only the concern of the farmer but of the physician and the people, for only fertile soil provides the proper balance of vitamins and minerals that we need in our food, and it affects not only the grains, vegetables, and fruit we eat, but, the livestock it nourishes in turn—and which we eat.

Unfortunately, so many of us have had only minimal nutrition through the years that we must now turn to taking supplements and vitamins to prevent deficiency diseases, especially subclinical ones.

The modern new science of nutritional therapy is slowly

being turned to, more and more, as an aid to the prevention of disease. It requires that we note not only the nutrient needs of the human body but the source and means by which this nutrition may be obtained. The body will perpetuate its good health if given foods which contain active, life-producing minerals and vitamins. It is never too late to change nutrition habits, but the younger you start, the quicker the results.

At present, packaged foods make up the greatest part of our diet. In most cases, these foods are devitalized, lacking in vitamins and minerals, so that in the end they are responsible for many of our illnesses. Whoever prepares the meals for the family actually is responsible for that family's well-being. If the family is fed with rich pastries, sugar-sweet puddings, deep-fried foods, fat meats, and canned foods, the mental and physical health of its members are bound to suffer. The penalties for poor nutrition are too-frequent colds, flu, fatigue, and a feeling of general malaise.

One does not have to be an especially talented gourmet cook or even one of that much-vaunted breed known as "born" cooks to be able to prepare healthful meals. By referring to the suggestions and recipes in this book and by using the ingredients listed in the various charts, with a bit of practice you will find you are giving your family added energy and health.

COOKING UTENSILS

It is a good idea to have certain basic equipment in the kitchen. A stainless steel steamer inset that fits into almost any size pot makes steaming your vegetables easy, and you'll enjoy them that much more for knowing they are so very much better for you than the ones with most of their vitamin and mineral content boiled out and washed down the drain in the water. A blender is particularly handy, and, if the budget will allow it, a juice machine is invaluable. Children —and grownups as well—will enjoy fresh vegetable and fruit juices, or a combination of both (for instance, celery-carrot-apple juice is delicious) in place of soda pop.

Pots and pans of stainless steel or enameled ironware are best. A preseasoned cast-iron skillet properly seasoned (a new one should be washed and dried, partly filled with oil, and slowly heated in the oven for an hour or two) needs only a drop or two of oil to keep eggs and most other foods from sticking, and is far better for health than a Teflon pan. A hamburger that is enriched with egg and wheat germ and seasoned to taste, sautéed lightly in such a skillet until medium rare, is delicious and gives you twice the protein of a plain grilled hamburger. With this you can serve a baked potato with plain yogurt and chives, and a fresh green salad. If you have a favorite bottled dressing, read the ingredients, then make one like it yourself, using apple-cider vinegar and an unsaturated oil such as safflower, or corn. (Of course, it will lack the additives of the commercial product.) Fresh fruit in season is always a good dessert.

COOKING BASICS

There is nothing more satisfying to the cook than producing a meal that is nourishing and delicious. This can also be good therapy. And adventure in the kitchen will never grow tedious if you experiment in your cooking.

Health-food stores carry all the specialized ingredients called for in the recipes that follow. With these recipes you can prepare meals to delight the palate and banish fatigue, for the ingredients are rich in nutrients that help new cells and retard aging.

Start with a batch of Fay Lavan's Mix (see the recipe below), and get into the habit of using this frequently. Add it to as many dishes as possible and watch your family's health improve.

FAY LAVAN'S MIX

¼ cup wheat germ
¼ cup dry skim milk (not the instant type) or high-protein powder
⅛ cup brewers' yeast
2 tablespoons calcium lactate
2 tablespoons gluconate

⅛ cup lecithin granules
⅛ cup soy powder
1 tablespoon rice polishings
1 ounce each of meal of sunflower seeds, pumpkin seeds, sesame seeds, chia seeds, almonds, and/or other nuts

Mix all ingredients well together. Store in a glass jar in the refrigerator. Add in small amounts, as desired, to your favorite recipes to enrich them nutritionally. (For instance, add about 4 tablespoons to each serving of cereal.)

NOTE: The amounts of the ingredients listed above are optional; you may vary both the amounts and the ingredients themselves, adding or substracting to make your own combinations and adjust the taste of the mix.

Balanced Menus

All recipes in the menus that carry an asterisk(*) can be located by referring to the Index.

I

Breakfast
Carrot-Celery-Apple Juice
Protein Energy Omelet*
1 Slice Whole Wheat Toast
Herb Tea or Decaffeinated Coffee with Milk

Luncheon
Crab Casserole*
Mixed Green Salad
Beverage

Dinner
Cream of Cauliflower-and-Mushroom Soup°
Low-Calorie Herbed Chicken°
Baked Carrots°
Brown Rice
Apple Brown Betty
Beverage

II

Breakfast
Cranberry-Apple-Grape Juice
Oatmeal (Fortified with Fay
Lavan's Mix°) and Milk
Cottage Cheese with Fruit
Beverage

Luncheon
Calf's Liver (breaded in Fay
Lavan's Mix°) Sautéed with
Onions
Mixed Green Salad
Half Grapefruit
Beverage

Dinner
Potassium Soup°
Veal Cutlets°
Whole Wheat or Artichoke Spaghetti with Tomato Sauce
Steamed Broccoli Sprinkled with Wheat Germ
Rhubarb Custard
Beverage

III

Breakfast
Orange-Pineapple-Papaya Juice
Scrambled Eggs (Fortified like
Protein Energy Omelet°)
Crisp Bacon or Sautéed Chicken
Livers
Beverage

Luncheon
Clam Casserole°
Alfred Lunt's Cold Rice Salad°
Half Cantaloupe
Beverage

Dinner
Nut Soup°
Meat Loaf°
Stewed Tomatoes
Fruit Pie
Beverage

IV

Breakfast
Grapefruit-Apricot-Black Cherry
  Juice
Corn Fritters*
Applesauce
Beverage

Luncheon
Salmon Croquettes*
Mixed Green Salad
Sliced Bananas with Milk
Beverage

Dinner
California Minestrone*
Steak
Broiled Mushrooms*
Sesame Asparagus*
Baked Potato with Yogurt and Chives
Fresh Fruit Cup
Beverage

V

Breakfast
Orange-Grapefruit-Pineapple
  Juice
Buckwheat Delight*
Cottage Cheese with Blueberries
Beverage

Luncheon
Beef-Eggplant Pie*
Mixed Green Salad
Applesauce
Beverage

Dinner
Vegetable-Oatmeal Soup*
Broiled Lamb Chops
Stuffed Sweet Potato*
Steamed Carrots
Rice Fruit Pudding
Beverage

VI

Breakfast
Papaya Juice mixed with Coco-
  nut Milk
Barley Pancakes*
Sautéed Chicken Livers
Beverage

Luncheon
Tuna Fish Salad
Marinated Asparagus*
Apple Cake*
Beverage

Dinner
Beef-Watercress Broth*
Baked Fish Breaded in Ground Wheat Germ
Zucchini Crisps*
Potatoes and Tomatoes*
Prune Gelatin
Beverage

ADDITIONAL DINNER MENUS FOR ONE WEEK

I

Chicken Cacciatore*
Brown Rice
Steamed Zucchini
Mixed Green Salad
Stewed Pears
Beverage

II

Mushroomburgers*
Green Beans
Creamed Corn
Watercress Salad
Apple Pudding
Beverage

III

Meat Loaf*
Spinach and Mushroom Salad
Baked Custard
Beverage

IV

Broiled Flank Steak
Broiled Tomatoes
Stuffed Sweet Potatoes*
Mixed Green Salad
Health Muffins*
Beverage

V

Corned Beef
Cabbage, Carrots, and Onions
  Cooked with the Beef
Alfred Lunt's Rice Salad*
Lemon Ice
Beverage

VI

Roast Leg of Lamb
Mashed Potatoes
Green Peas
Avocado Salad
Pineapple Nut Torte*
Beverage

VII

Double-Good Macaroni and
  Cheese*
Asparagus
Wilted Cucumber Salad
Gelatin Dessert
Beverage

Main Course Dishes

Try to substitute wheat germ for bread crumbs, wherever they are called for, seasoning them with your favorite herbs. This is a good trick whether you are preparing plain hamburgers or a casserole calling for a topping of bread crumbs. Dredge fillets of fish (or chicken breasts or ground beef shaped like hot dogs) with herbed wheat germ mixed with sunflower- or pumpkin-seed meal before sautéeing them.

The goodness of ground organ meats combines well with highly nutritious brewers' yeast, wheat germ, and high-protein powder to make dishes that are not only rich in nutritional value but irresistible to the young crowd. You have only to shape them into hamburger patties or facsimiles of hot dogs and seasoned to taste. Try them seasoned à la pizza. Another way to bridge the generation gap!

Cooked-meat patties prepared this way are packed with protein. Just add a salad and you will have a meal.

It's wise, when you are preparing meat loaves, to make two—one for now and one for the freezer. That way, when you need it, you can take it out and pop it into the oven to warm through. It's a nice way to say "welcome!" to unexpected guests who stay for dinner.

All of the nutrition-packed main dishes that follow have a zesty goodness your family will enjoy. Each of these hearty and healthful recipes can double as a side dish, and they're great to serve at a buffet.

BEEF EGGPLANT PIE

2 pounds very lean ground beef
1 medium eggplant
2 large onions, diced
½ cup tomato puree
2 cups dry red wine
1 cup unsulfured raisins

1 clove garlic, crushed
cold-pressed oil, as needed
1 teaspoon cinnamon
sea salt and pepper to taste
wheat germ (about ½ cup)

Brown the beef in a very small amount of fat in a hot saucepan; remove from pan, draining as much of the excess fat as possible. Sauté onions; add to meat with tomato puree, wine, raisins, garlic, and all seasonings.

Slice eggplant thin; sauté in oil. Place in a large greased casserole in alternate layers with wheat germ and meat, starting and ending with wheat germ. Bake, uncovered, in a preheated oven at 350°F. for 30 minutes.

Serves 6.

MEAT LOAF

1 pound ground lean beef (or half beef and half organ meats)
2 large eggs
3 tablespoons soy milk
1 teaspoon bone meal
2 tablespoons brewers' yeast

1 cup sunflower meal
½ cup minced onion
1 teaspoon dolomite
½ teaspoon fresh sage
1 teaspoon kelp
½ teaspoon sea salt
¼ teaspoon pepper

Put all ingredients except meat into blender; blend well. Add to the meat and mix thoroughly. Pack into lightly greased loaf pan and bake in a preheated oven at 300°F. for about 1 hour.

Serves 4.

114   *Cooking for Health*

Variations

1. Substitute tomato puree for soy milk.
2. Add chopped olives and pimento.
3. Add chopped pickle.
4. Add ½ cup ground carrots.
5. Put a row of hard-boiled eggs through middle of meat loaf.
6. Put a 1-inch layer of sliced parboiled parsnips in bottom of loaf pan.
7. Place a layer of meat in pan, add a layer of sliced parboiled parsnips, and then a final layer of meat.
8. Prepare as in number 7, substituting green pepper for parsnips.

HOT DOGS A LA NUTRITION

1 pound ground meat (lung and heart mixed with chuck, round, or neck meat)
2 medium-size carrots, grated
1 onion, finely minced
1 tablespoon brewers' yeast
1 tablespoon wheat germ
1 egg, beaten
pinch each of thyme, marjoram, and oregano
salt and pepper to taste
1 teaspoon kelp
ground sesame seeds and soy flour (for coating)

Mix together all the ingredients except the sesame seeds and soy flour. Divide into 4 portions; shape each like a hot dog and roll in the combined sesame seeds and soy flour. Broil, turning once, and serve hot with any good, ready-made tomato sauce.

Serves 4.

MUSHROOMBURGERS

½ pound mushrooms, finely
    chopped
½ pound ground beef round

sea salt and pepper to taste
garlic powder to taste

Combine all ingredients and shape into thick patties. Broil, turning once.

Serves 3.

Variations

1. For a Middle-Eastern touch, substitute cumin for garlic.
2. For a nutritional bonus, use ⅓ pound each finely chopped mushrooms, ground round, and ground lung or heart (instead of half mushrooms and half beef).

VEAL CUTLETS

4 veal cutlets
1 egg, beaten
½ cup wheat germ
1 tablespoon brewers' yeast

⅛ teaspoon each of marjoram,
    thyme, basil, and oregano
¼ teaspoon paprika
cold-pressed oil, as needed

Combine wheat germ and seasonings. Dip cutlets into beaten egg, then into wheat-germ mixture; sauté lightly in oil on each side until golden brown. Or place on an oiled baking sheet and bake in a preheated oven at 350°F. for 20 minutes.

Serves 2.

NOTE: This is also good served with a good, prepared tomato sauce.

CHICKEN CACCIATORE

1 frying chicken (about 3 pounds), cut into serving pieces
1 clove garlic, peeled
¼ cup unbleached whole-grain flour or wheat-germ flour
¼ cup olive or salad oil
2¼ cups cooked or canned tomatoes

1 can tomato paste
6 small white onions, peeled
1 tablespoon minced parsley
1 bay leaf
1 teaspoon salt
dash pepper (optional)

Wash the chicken pieces; dry well. (Save neck and giblets to make soup for another meal.) Rub well with garlic, then mince garlic and set aside. Combine flour and 1 teaspoon salt in a paper bag, put in the chicken pieces and shake until they are well coated. Heat oil in a Dutch oven, add the chicken pieces, a few at a time; brown on all sides, then drain well on paper towels. Pour off fat remaining in pot before returning the browned chicken to it. Add the minced garlic, tomatoes, tomato paste, onions, and bay leaf. Simmer covered, shaking the pot occasionally, until chicken is tender (about 1 hour).

Serves 4.

CHICKEN CUTLETS

4 chicken breasts
1 egg, beaten
sea salt and pepper to taste
1 cup (approximately) wheat germ

1 clove garlic, crushed
pinch of oregano
cold-pressed oil for sautéing

Have the chicken breasts boned, skinned, and cut into 2 pieces each (to make 8 pieces); pound each piece until fairly flat. Sprinkle with salt and pepper, dip into beaten egg, then into wheat germ seasoned with garlic and oregano. Sauté in cold-pressed oil until done. Drain and serve immediately.

Serves 8.

BRAISED CHICKEN WITH VEGETABLES AND EGGS

1 3-pound broiler or fryer, cut up	1½ cups thinly sliced carrots
½ cup whole wheat pastry flour	1½ cups thinly sliced celery
1 teaspoon salt	¾ cup finely chopped onion
¼ teaspoon pepper	¾ cup diced green pepper
3 tablespoons oil	4 hard-cooked eggs, chopped
¾ cup water	2 cups cooked hot brown rice

Combine flour, salt, and pepper. Coat the chicken pieces with this mixture, then brown in a Dutch oven in hot oil. Add the water, cover the pot tightly, and cook for 30 minutes. Add the vegetables; cook for another 30 minutes. Remove from heat. Fold in the chopped eggs. Heat through, and serve over the rice.

Serves 4.

LOW-CALORIE HERBED CHICKEN

1 4-pound (approximately) chicken	1 teaspoon thyme
1 carrot	1 teaspoon tarragon
2 celery stalks	1 can beef bouillon
several sprigs parsley	salt and pepper to taste

Wash and dry the chicken. Into the cavity insert the carrot (cut lengthwise into quarters), celery, and parsley. Twist wingtips of the chicken under back; tie legs together. Place chicken on its back in a baking pan and roast in a preheated oven at 400°F. for 15 minutes, then lower oven temperature to 375° and start basting-seasoning procedure: baste with bouillon; sprinkle wtih a little of the thyme and tarragon. Continue to baste and sprinkle with herbs every 15 minutes for about 1¼ hours, or until chicken is well done.

Serves 4.

BAKED CHICKEN SALAD

2 cups cooked diced chicken	2 tablespoons lemon juice
1½ cups thinly sliced celery	½ cup grated natural cheese
½ cup chopped almonds	salt and pepper to taste
2 teaspoons minced onion	3 hard-cooked eggs
1 cup mayonnaise	parsley for garnish

Combine all the ingredients except eggs and parsley, and pile lightly into buttered casserole or 4 individual baking dishes. Sprinkle with cheese; bake in a preheated oven at 375°F. for 25 minutes. Top with a layer of finely chopped egg white and sieved yolk; garnish with parsley. Serve hot. Serves 4.

CHOW MEIN

1 cup sliced onions, cut length-wise	2½ cups thinly sliced celery, cut crosswise
3 tablespoons oil	3 cups fresh bean sprouts
1 pound cooked pork or chicken, cut into strips	3 tablespoons cornstarch or arrowroot
1 can bamboo shoots, drained and cut into fine strips	6 tablespoons soy sauce
¼ cup sliced mushrooms (canned or fresh)	¾ cup beef bouillon
	dash of ginger

Sauté onions in 1 tablespoon of the oil until golden; remove from pan to large bowl. In the same pan, in another table-spoon of the oil, sauté the meat. Place the third tablespoon of oil in a different pan and sauté the bamboo shoots and mushrooms in it; remove them to a bowl, then sauté the celery in this same pan. (NOTE: All the vegetables must be crisp; this is the Chinese way of cooking and does not destroy nutrients.)

Combine the sautéed vegetables and meat; add the bean sprouts. Over low heat, in another saucepan, mix together well the cornstarch (or arrowroot), soy sauce, ginger, and bouillon. Add to meat mixture, stirring in carefully so as not to break up bean sprouts. Continue to stir until mixture bubbles. Serve immediately with boiled soy noodles or brown rice.

Serves 6.

CROQUETTES

4 ounces salmon or other fish, chicken, or leftover meat
1 onion, chopped
1 green pepper, chopped
1 small clove garlic, minced (or ½ teaspoon garlic powder)
1 egg
4 tablespoons wheat germ or Fay Lavan's Mix (see Index)
salt and pepper to taste
vegetable oil for frying
enough extra wheat germ to coat patties

Put onion, green pepper, garlic, egg, 4 tablespoons wheat germ, salt, and pepper into blender until well blended; mix with fish or meat; shape into patties. Roll in wheat germ; sauté in oil until lightly browned on both sides.

Serves 2.

CLAM CASSEROLE

2 cans clams, minced and drained
3 tablespoons butter
3 tablespoons rice flour
1 cup liquid (juice from the clams with milk added to make this amount)
salt and pepper to taste
seasoned bread crumbs or wheat germ
½ cup grated cheese (optional)
additional butter as needed

Melt the 3 tablespoons butter and add rice flour to it, stirring constantly to make a smooth paste. Add milk-and-clam-juice mixture and continue to stir over medium heat until sauce has thickened. Add clams, mix well. Pour into buttered casserole and cover with bread crumbs or wheat germ. Sprinkle with cheese and dot with butter, if you like. Bake in a preheated oven at 400°F. for about 20 minutes, or until brown and crusty on top.

Serves 4.

CRAB CASSEROLE

1 pound fresh crab, or 2 7½-ounce cans crab meat

2 cups whole wheat bread crumbs

2 tablespoons chopped pickle relish (optional)

¼ cup chopped pimento

½ cup chopped green olives

1 6½-ounce (or larger) can mushrooms, drained

1 cup grated sharp Cheddar cheese

dash of paprika

WHITE SAUCE

4 tablespoons butter or margarine or oil

¼ cup unbleached white flour

3 cups milk

¾ teaspoon salt

⅛ teaspoon pepper

To prepare the white sauce, melt butter in a saucepan, work in flour to make a smooth paste. Add milk gradually, stirring constantly to prevent mixture from lumping. Cook until thickened; stir in salt and pepper. Remove from heat.

Combine all other ingredients except cheese and paprika and add to sauce. Turn into a greased casserole; bake in a preheated oven at 350°F. for 20 minutes, then sprinkle cheese over top. Return to oven and bake for another 10 minutes. Sprinkle with paprika before serving. Serves 6.

DOUBLE-GOOD MACARONI AND CHEESE

8 ounces soya or whole wheat macaroni

1 pound cream-style cottage cheese

1 cup dairy sour cream

1 fertile egg, beaten

1 teaspoon sea salt

⅛ teaspoon freshly ground black pepper

1 tablespoon grated onion

1 to 3 tablespoons brewers' yeast

½ pound Cheddar cheese, grated (optional)

¼ cup wheat germ (optional)

Cook and drain macaroni. In a large bowl, combine the remaining ingredients except Cheddar cheese and wheat germ, mix lightly until blended, then fold in macaroni. Spoon into a greased 9-inch square pan or individual casseroles. If desired, top with the Cheddar cheese or wheat germ. Bake in a preheated oven at 350°F. for about 45 minutes, or until bubbly and lightly browned. Serves 8.

MEATLESS HAMBURGERS

2 cups farmer cheese
1 cup whole wheat bread crumbs
¾ teaspoon salt or ground kelp
pepper to taste
1 tablespoon finely chopped green pepper

2 tablespoons finely chopped onion
1 egg, slightly beaten
2½ teaspoons ground seeds or nuts
butter or oil for frying

Set aside ½ cup of the bread crumbs. Combine all the other ingredients except the fat for frying; shape the mixture into 8 cakes; coat these thoroughly in the reserved crumbs. Brown on both sides in hot butter or oil. Serve immediately with any good ready-made tomato sauce.

Serves 4.

QUICK ONION SOUFFLÉ

1 jar boiled onions
⅓ cup onion liquid (from the jar)
4 tablespoons butter or margarine
4 tablespoons flour

⅓ cup milk or cream
3 egg yolks
salt and pepper to taste (optional)
4 egg whites
pinch of salt

Drain onions well and chop fine. Reserve the liquid (adding water to it, if necessary, to make the ⅓ cup called for).

Make a cream sauce as follows: Melt the butter in a saucepan and blend in the flour, stirring constantly until well blended. Add the onion juice and milk or cream, stirring all the while. When the mixture begins to thicken, add the egg yolks, 1 at a time, beating each in thoroughly. Season with salt and pepper. Remove from heat. Add chopped onions.

Beat the egg whites until stiff but not dry, adding the pinch of salt to them. Stir a good spoonful of the whites into the onion-yolk mixture, then carefully fold in the remaining whites. Turn into a buttered soufflé dish and bake for about 30 minutes in a preheated oven at 375°F.

Serves 4.

MUSHROOM-STUFFED CABBAGE

1 head cabbage	3 tablespoons cold-pressed oil
½ pound mushrooms, sliced	1 cup canned tomatoes, strained
½ cup chopped onions	1 teaspoon (or more) sea salt
½ cup brown rice	

Cover the cabbage with boiling water and let stand for 10 minutes to soften, then carefully remove 16 leaves. Heat 1 tablespoon of the oil in a skillet and sauté the mushroom and onions in it for about 10 minutes. Turn into a bowl with the rice and 1 teaspoon salt; mix well. Put a rounded table-spoonful of the mixture onto each leaf, folding the leaf up over it and then wrapping the sides and top like an envelope.

Place the rolls in a good-sized pot. Add tomatoes, additional salt (if desired), and balance of the oil. Cover, and let simmer for 45 minutes.

Makes 16 rolls.

Soups

All these soups are different and hearty, and with a salad and bread and butter, will make a satisfying meal.

BASIC VEGETABLE PUREE

This can be used as a base for all cream soups, or can be mixed with equal parts of chicken or beef stock. It can also be utilized, like stock, in some sauces. There is no one un-alterable instruction on how to prepare it; you are free to make your own proportions and combinations. Where possible, leave the skin on the vegetables that go into this, peeling only those with a heavy skin (like potatoes). Vary the seasonings as well as the vegetables: use thyme, marjoram, basil, among others; salt and pepper to taste.

Basically, combine:

potatoes	celery	string beans
onions	green pepper	peas
cabbage	squash	parsley
carrots		

Cut the larger vegetables, such as potatoes, into chunks; shred the cabbage. Cook all together in a steamer. When the vegetables are done, puree in a blender, using the liquid from the steamer. The puree will be fairly thick. Refrigerate, and use as needed. This will keep without spoiling for one week.

MAINE CLAM CHOWDER

1 quart or 2 large cans clams, chopped	1 onion, chopped
	1 quart milk, scalded
¼ pound salt pork	¼ cup (approximately) oil
1 quart (4 cups) diced potatoes	salt and pepper to taste

Remove black parts from clams. Reserve the liquid. Cut the pork into small pieces and fry in hot oil until crisp and golden, then remove from pan; discard fat.

Simmer potatoes and onion for 30 minutes in milk to which the clam liquid has been added. Add clams and pork bits. Season with salt and pepper.

Serves 4.

BEEF-WATERCRESS BROTH

2 beef shanks	2 to 4 garlic cloves, chopped
1½ quarts water	1 bunch watercress, chopped
2 onions, chopped	salt and pepper to taste

Boil the shanks in the water for 30 minutes; skim residue. Add half the onions and garlic; let simmer for 1 hour. Add the rest of the onions and garlic and simmer for another 30 minutes. Remove from heat and strain. Add watercress; season; simmer 15 minutes longer.

Serves 6.

CALIFORNIA MINESTRONE

1 cup dried navy or other white beans	1 cup coarsely chopped cabbage
6 cups cold water	2 tablespoons minced parsley
1 onion, minced	1 cup tomato sauce
1 clove garlic, minced	2 cups bouillon
2 stalks celery, minced	1 teaspoon salt
¼ cup salad oil	¼ teaspoon pepper
½ cup brown rice	grated Parmesan cheese

Soak beans in water overnight; cover, and bring to a boil in water in which they were soaked. Reduce heat and simmer until tender.

Lightly brown onion, garlic, and celery in oil; add to beans with all remaining ingredients except cheese. Simmer for 40 minutes longer. Serve topped with cheese.

Serves 6.

CREAM OF CAULIFLOWER-AND-MUSHROOM SOUP

1 cup raw certified milk	1 small can mushrooms
½ cup water	1 teaspoon minced parsley
1 small head cauliflower	salt and pepper to taste

Break cauliflower into flowerets. Put all ingredients except parsley into blender and blend thoroughly. Pour puree into saucepan and heat to boiling. Add parsley and serve.

Serves 4.

CREAM OF WATERCRESS-AND-POTATO SOUP

3 cups warm water
1 cup fresh watercress, chopped fine
1 medium potato, peeled and diced
½ cup powdered skim milk

1 teaspoon ground kelp (optional)
½ teaspoon paprika
¼ teaspoon oregano
¼ cup chopped onion
salt and pepper to taste

Combine all the ingredients in a saucepan and cook over low heat about 30 minutes or until potato is tender.

Serves 4.

CELERY SOUP

1 bunch celery, chopped
1 small onion, chopped
1 pint milk
1 pint water

1 tablespoon whole wheat flour
salt and pepper to taste
dash of nutmeg (optional)

Cook celery and onion together in a steamer for 15 minutes or until tender. Mix the flour with a little of the milk and water, and when flour is completely dissolved, stir into the rest of the milk and water which have been mixed together. Add the celery and onion; cook over low heat for 15 or 20 minutes.

If you prefer a smooth soup, you may put the celery-onion mixture through a colander or potato ricer, or run in a blender until smooth, then blend into the milk-and-water mixture, and proceed to cook as above. Season to taste, blending in nutmeg, if desired.

Serves 4.

VEGETABLE-OATMEAL SOUP

1 cup chopped carrots
½ cup chopped onion
2 tablespoons butter
½ cup instant oatmeal
4 cups chicken broth or bouillon
  from cubes

3 tablespoons lemon juice
½ teaspoon salt
  dash of pepper
1 tablespoon chopped parsley

Brown carrots and onion lightly in butter; add oatmeal, stirring for 2 minutes; add broth, lemon juice, and salt and pepper. Bring mixture to a boil, then lower the heat and simmer for 3 to 5 minutes longer. Sprinkle with parsley, and serve.

Serves 6.

POTASSIUM SOUP

1 bunch parsley
1 bunch celery, chopped
4 to 5 zucchini, sliced
½ pound green beans
½ teaspoon each of sage, rosemary, sweet basil

pinch onion salt
salt and pepper to taste
4 tablespoons butter

Reserve enough of the parsley to make 1 tablespoon when it is minced, and reserve this to use as a garnish. Place the balance of the parsley in a large pot with the celery, zucchini, green beans, and enough water to cover; bring to a boil; reduce the heat and simmer for 30 minutes. Strain, then puree the vegetables in a blender and return to the strained broth, mixing all well together. Add the seasoning and butter, stirring latter in over heat until it melts. Garnish with minced parsley before serving.

Serves 6.

NOTE: This soup is also excellent to serve to someone who is ill. The seasonings can then be omitted.

NUT SOUP

½ onion, chopped
2 tablespoons peanut oil
1 tablespoon rice flour
1½ tablespoons brewers' yeast
½ cup peanut butter

2 cups milk
2 cups tomato juice
salt and pepper to taste
minced chives for garnish

Sauté onion in oil until transparent. Thoroughly blend in flour, brewers' yeast, and peanut butter, in that order. Add milk gradually, a little at a time, stirring constantly so mixture remains smooth, and cook over low heat, stirring all the while until mixture thickens and comes to a boil. Add tomato juice and salt and pepper, and let soup come just to boiling point once again. Garnish with chives and serve.
Serves 6.

SCOTCH BROTH

2½ cups light vegetable stock or
water
½ cup yellow split peas
½ cup barley
1 carrot, chopped

½ cup chopped celery
1 small leek, chopped
1 tablespoon chopped parsley
salt and pepper to taste
2 teaspoons finely grated carrot

Bring vegetable stock (or water) to a boil, then add split peas and barley; simmer gently for 1 hour. Add all other ingredients except grated carrot, and continue to cook over medium heat until broth is thick, stirring occasionally so barley does not stick or scorch. If soup becomes too thick, thin with a little more water or stock. Garnish with grated carrots just before serving.
Serves 4.

SPLIT PEA SOUP

¼ pound salt pork, or bone from
  baked ham
2 cups dried split peas
½ cup chopped celery
2 onions, chopped
3 cloves garlic
3 quarts water

1 teaspoon thyme
¼ teaspoon oregano
¼ teaspoon pepper
  salt to taste
  sour cream (optional)
  chopped parsley (optional)

Cook the pork or hambone in water with split peas, celery,
onions, and garlic for about 2 hours over low heat, or until
peas are tender. Stir in seasonings. Remove pieces of pork
or hambone. Serve topped with a dollop of sour cream or a
little chopped parsley on each portion, and with buttered
croutons.

Serves 6 to 8.

HOT CHICKEN AND EGG DROP SOUP

1 large cooked chicken breast
2 cups bean sprouts
6 cups chicken stock

3 eggs
1 teaspoon soy sauce

Skin and bone the chicken, and shred the meat. Heat the
stock to boiling, and add shredded chicken and bean sprouts
to it. Cook gently for about 5 minutes. Beat the eggs with
soy sauce and add in a thin stream to the hot soup, stirring
constantly.

Serves 6.

Side Dishes

TOMATO PILAF

3 cups fresh tomato juice
2 medium-size onions, diced
1½ cups brown rice

1½ teaspoons sea salt
   dash of pepper (optional)
2 tablespoons cold-pressed oil

Sauté onions in oil in a saucepan over very low heat until transparent. Add rice, and sauté until it is opaque. Neither onions nor rice should be at all browned. In a separate saucepan, bring tomato juice, seasoned with salt (and pepper) to a boil, then add to rice mixture. Cover, and let simmer slowly until all liquid is absorbed. *Do not stir.* Remove from heat and uncover. Place a paper towel over the saucepan (to absorb excess moisture), then replace the lid. Allow to sit undisturbed for 15 minutes before serving.

Serves 4.

Variation

For Spanish style, sauté 1 chopped green pepper with the onion, add a pinch of saffron, and season generously with garlic powder.

SUPER PILAF

1 cup brown rice
1 cup sliced fresh mushrooms
1 medium-size onion, finely
   chopped
2½ cups water or chicken broth
½ cup chopped apricots

⅓ cup almonds or pignolia nuts
⅓ cup raisins
1 teaspoon cinnamon
   sea salt and pepper to taste
   cold-pressed oil as needed

Sauté onion and mushrooms in oil in a medium-size saucepan until mushrooms are soft and onion is transparent. Remove to a covered dish to keep warm. In the same pan,

129

sauté the rice until it becomes opaque. Do not allow it to brown or burn. Bring the water (or broth) to a boil and add to the rice, then add all the other ingredients. *Do not stir*. Cover the pot and let simmer at low heat until all liquid is absorbed (30 to 45 minutes). Remove from heat and uncover.

Stir the mixture carefully, then place a paper towel over the saucepan (to absorb extra moisture) and replace the lid. Let stand undisturbed for 15 minutes before serving.

Serves 3.

CHINESE VEGETABLE MEDLEY

½ teaspoon honey
¾ cup chicken stock
2 tablespoons soy sauce
1 tablespoon cornstarch
¼ cup cold-pressed oil
    pinch of sea salt
1 clove garlic, minced

2 slices shredded fresh ginger
1 medium onion, sliced
3 red radishes, sliced very thin
½ cup sliced fresh mushrooms
½ cup diced celery
1 cup shredded Chinese cabbage
1 cup snow peas

Mix together honey, chicken stock, soy sauce, and cornstarch, and set aside. Heat up a dry saucepan until very hot, then add the oil and salt; turn the heat to medium and brown the garlic and ginger, stirring constantly. Add the onion and stir fry for about 1 minute. Turn the heat to high again and add radishes, mushrooms, celery, and Chinese cabbage, and stir fry just until vegetables are tender. Add snow peas, and then the sauce mixture. Cook, stirring all the while, until the sauce thickens and becomes glossy, then remove from the heat. Serve immediately over hot brown rice.

Serves 4.

DELIGHTFUL DUMPLINGS

1 yeast cake
⅓ cup buttermilk
2 eggs
¼ cup oil

½ cup rice polishings
½ teaspoon salt
3 tablespoons wheat germ

Heat buttermilk until warm and dissolve the yeast in it; cool.
Blend with the eggs and oil. Stir in rice polishings, salt,
and wheat germ. Let batter stand, covered, in a warm place
until it rises (for about 1 hour). Stir down. Drop by spoonfuls into steamer. Steam, covered, for 5 minutes, then uncover the steamer and cook for another 10 minutes.

Makes 12 dumplings. (Allow 2 dumplings per serving,
and serve in place of potatoes, rice, or pasta.)

ALFRED LUNT'S COLD RICE SALAD

6 cups water
2 cups rice
6 green onions, chopped
1 4-ounce jar pimentos
½ pint cherry tomatoes
½ green pepper, chopped

DRESSING

1 clove garlic
½ cup cold-pressed oil
¼ cup lemon juice
salt to taste

Bring the water to a brisk boil. Add the rice and cook, covered, at a rolling boil for about 20 minutes or until done,
stirring occasionally to prevent sticking. Drain immediately
in a large colander and wash thoroughly under cold running
water.

To prepare the dressing, puree garlic in a press and mix
with oil, lemon juice, and salt. Combine the rice with the
onions, pimentos, tomatoes, and green pepper. Pour on the
dressing, and toss.

Serves 6.

MARINATED ASPARAGUS

12 asparagus spears (frozen or fresh)
2 tablespoons olive oil
2 tablespoons cider vinegar
¼ teaspoon sea salt
1 teaspoon honey
1 bay leaf, crushed fine

Steam asparagus until tender and crisp, and place in a shallow dish; drain. Beat together oil, vinegar, sea salt and honey; mix in bay leaf. Pour over the asparagus; cover the dish and refrigerate for several hours, turning the spears once. Remove from refrigerator about 20 minutes before serving.

SESAME ASPARAGUS

2 10-ounce packages frozen asparagus spears or 1 bunch fresh asparagus
1 tablespoon sesame seeds

Cook frozen asparagus according to the package directions (or steam washed fresh asparagus, after breaking off the lower tough part, in lightly salted water until tender—about 12 to 15 minutes). Meantime, toast the sesame seeds in a small frying pan over low heat until they are golden brown, shaking the pan often so the seeds do not scorch. Drain the asparagus and sprinkle with the seeds just before serving.
Serves 6.

POPPY SEED BEANS

2 cups green beans, cut diagon-
ally
2 tablespoons butter
1 tablespoon lemon juice

2 tablespoons poppy seeds or
roasted, salted sunflower-
seed kernels
dill salt to taste

Cook or steam the beans in as little water as possible until tender; drain. Gently mix in butter, lemon juice, and poppy seeds (or sunflower-seed kernels).

Serves 3 to 4.

RED CABBAGE AND MUNG BEAN SPROUTS SAUTÉ

3 tablespoons safflower oil
4 cups shredded red cabbage
2 cups mung bean sprouts

1 tablespoon caraway seeds
sea salt
freshly ground pepper

Heat the oil in a large, cast-iron skillet and sauté the cabbage and mung bean sprouts for about 5 minutes (vegetables should be tender-crisp). Add caraway seeds. Season to taste with salt and pepper; toss lightly. Serve hot.

Serves 6.

CARROT PANCAKES

1 large carrot, shredded
1 large potato, cut into small
pieces
1 small onion, diced
1 large egg

1 tablespoon wheat germ
1 tablespoon soya flour
sea salt to taste
dash of ground basil
cold-pressed oil for frying

Put the vegetables into a blender and blend thoroughly. Blend in all the other ingredients except the oil. Heat the oil in a large cast-iron skillet and drop the batter by table-spoonfuls into it. Cook the pancakes at low heat to avoid scorching; when brown on one side, turn and brown the other side. Drain on paper toweling, and serve immediately.

Serves 4.

BAKED CARROTS

6 medium-size carrots, coarsely   1 cup dry whole wheat bread
   ground or grated   crumbs
1 medium-size onion, chopped   ¼ cup butter or oil
3 eggs, beaten   salt to taste
2 cups milk

Mix together well all the ingredients; turn into a greased
1-quart casserole. Bake in a preheated oven at 350°F. for
about 45 minutes.

    Serves 4 to 6.

CARROTS WITH TARRAGON AND CREAM

4 cups peeled and sliced carrots   2 tablespoons cream
2 tablespoons butter   ½ teaspoon dried leaf tarragon
2 tablespoons water   salt and pepper to taste
1 tablespoon honey

Melt butter in a saucepan. Add the sliced carrots, water, and
honey; cover, and cook over low heat 10 to 15 minutes, or
until carrots are just tender. Add the cream, tarragon, salt,
and pepper. Cook uncovered for another 1 or 2 minutes.

    Serves 4.

HONEY-GLAZED CARROTS

4 medium-size carrots   2 tablespoons honey
¼ cup (approximately) water   2 tablespoons butter
½ teaspoon salt or salt substitute   dash of nutmeg

Peel the carrots and cut them into sticks. Place with the
water and salt in a small saucepan and cook for about 10
minutes (there should be no liquid left). Add salt. In another small pan, heat honey and butter together until butter
is melted; blend the mixture and spoon over the cooked
carrots. Heat gently at low heat, shaking the pan constantly, until the carrots are well glazed. Sprinkle with the
nutmeg; serve immediately.

    Serves 3.

PIZZAED CARROTS

fresh carrots
tomato juice

oregano
grated Parmesan cheese

Scrub carrots and cut them into pieces; place in a pot and pour over enough tomato juice to just cover; sprinkle with oregano. Cover the pot and cook at high heat till mixture boils; reduce heat; let simmer for no more than 5 minutes. Uncover; sprinkle with cheese; replace the lid and let stand for a few minutes without cooking. Uncover again and stir (to blend cheese through); add more cheese on top, and serve.

CELERY-ALMOND CASSEROLE

3 cups sliced celery
¼ cup slivered almonds
1 tablespoon butter
½ can celery soup
1 cup drained cooked peas

½ cup grated Cheddar cheese
½ cup buttered whole wheat bread crumbs or wheat germ
salt and pepper to taste

Cook celery in a small amount of boiling salted water until barely tender. In a separate saucepan, lightly brown the almonds in the butter; stir in the celery soup and peas. Season with salt and pepper.

Place half the cooked celery in a greased 1-quart casserole and top with half the almond mixture; sprinkle half the cheese over this. Repeat this process: a layer of celery, a layer of almond mixture, balance of cheese. Top the whole with the bread crumbs. Bake in a preheated oven at 350°F. for 20 minutes or until bubbly.

Serves 6.

CURRIED CELERY AND MUSHROOMS

3 cups diced or sliced celery
½ cup chopped onion
¼ teaspoon salt
¼ cup vinegar or white wine
½ cup hot water
1 cup (approximately) milk
1 bouillon cube

5 tablespoons butter
½ pound mushrooms, sliced
1 teaspoon lemon juice
1 tablespoon whole wheat pastry
      flour
½ teaspoon curry powder
   salt and pepper to taste

Combine celery, onion, salt, vinegar (or wine) and water in a pot; bring to a boil, then lower the heat and simmer a few minutes longer (only until the celery is tender). Drain, reserving the liquid. Measure the liquid and add enough milk to it to make 1¼ cups, then add the bouillon cube.

Melt 3 tablespoons of the butter in saucepan and sauté the mushrooms lightly in it for 5 minutes. Sprinkle with the lemon juice; set aside. Melt the 2 remaining tablespoons butter in another saucepan; blend in the flour and curry powder, then slowly stir in the milk mixture. Cook over moderate heat, stirring constantly, until smooth and thickened. Fold in the cooked celery and mushrooms. Season to taste with salt and pepper.

Serves 6 to 8.

EGGPLANT MÉLANGE

6 tablespoons peanut oil
1 medium-size eggplant, peeled
      and finely chopped
1 cup chopped onion
3 fresh tomatoes, chopped

1 teaspoon dried crushed basil
   salt and pepper to taste
1 heaping tablespoon yogurt
1 heaping tablespoon sour cream
1 heaping tablespoon mayonnaise

Heat the oil in a skillet, then add eggplant and onion. Cook over low heat until tender, turning mixture frequently with pancake turner. When eggplant is soft, add the tomatoes, basil, and salt and pepper. When the tomatoes are hot through but not really cooked, stir in the yogurt, sour cream, and mayonnaise. Heat but do not boil.

Serves 4.

EGGPLANT PATTIES

1 medium-size eggplant
¼ cup (approximately) water
2 cups ground walnuts
½ cup wheat germ
2 teaspoons sea salt

1 medium-size onion, chopped
2 eggs, beaten
1 tablespoon chopped parsley
pepper to taste (optional)
oil as needed

Peel and slice the eggplant; cook in the water until tender (about 15 minutes); let cool. Drain and mash, then mix with all the other ingredients except the oil. Shape into patties.

Heat the oil in a heavy skillet; sauté patties over medium heat, turning once, to a golden brown. Drain on paper towels.

Makes 6 or 7 4-inch patties.

EGGPLANT STACKS

1 medium-size eggplant
1 egg, beaten
salt and pepper
3 tablespoons sesame or safflower
oil

½ pound (approximately) raw-milk Swiss cheese, thinly sliced
sesame seeds
wheat germ

Cut the eggplant into ¼-inch-thick slices; sprinkle each with salt, stack the slices in a bowl, and cover with a heavy plate; let stand for 30 minutes. Wash and dry the slices.

Heat the oil in a heavy skillet. Dip the eggplant slices into the beaten egg (which has been seasoned with salt and pepper) and fry on one side for 2 minutes; turn. Sprinkle each eggplant slice with sesame seeds and wheat germ, and top with a slice of Swiss cheese; fry on the second side until both eggplant and cheese are soft (about 3 minutes). As they are done, stack the eggplant slices, cheese side up, in a shallow pan. Just before serving, place for about 5 minutes in an oven preheated to 400°F.

Serves 2.

BROILED MUSHROOMS

1 pound large mushrooms   soy sauce
  butter   grated Cheddar cheese

Wash the mushrooms; drain well. Carefully remove their stems. Place the caps, hollow side up, into a shallow greased baking pan or on a greased cookie sheet. Into each mushroom put a dab of butter, 2 drops of soy sauce, and a sprinkling of cheese. Broil until butter and cheese are sizzling.

SCALLOPED POTATOES WITH COTTAGE CHEESE

1 cup thinly sliced raw potatoes   salt and pepper to taste
1 cup creamed cottage cheese   1 tablespoon butter
1 tablespoon minced onion   ½ cup (approximately) milk

Butter a 1-quart baking dish. Arrange alternate layers of potatoes and cottage cheese in it, seasoning each layer with minced onion, and salt and pepper. Dot each layer with butter. Pour the milk over all (it should cover the potatoes). Bake in a preheated moderate oven (350°F.) for about 45 minutes, or until potatoes are tender.
    Serves 3.

POTATOES AND TOMATOES

2 medium potatoes, peeled and   ½ teaspoon turmeric
  cubed   ⅛ teaspoon powdered ginger
1 large onion, diced   1½ teaspoons sea salt
2 large tomatoes, chopped   3 tablespoons vegetable oil
1 teaspoon minced fresh green
  chili

Heat the oil in a saucepan, then sauté the potatoes, onion, and chili in it for about 5 minutes. Reduce the heat. Blend in the ginger and turmeric; add the tomatoes and salt; mix well. Simmer until the potatoes are cooked, adding water as needed so there is some sauce. Serve with meat or fish.
    Serves 2 to 3.

SPINACH WITH CREAM CHEESE

1 package frozen chopped spinach or 2 pounds fresh spinach, thoroughly washed and
chopped fine
1 3-ounce package cream cheese

1 clove garlic, minced or whole
dash of nutmeg
dash of high-protein powder
salt and pepper to taste

Cook the spinach, using as little water as possible (there should be no liquid left when spinach is done). Add cream cheese and garlic, stirring constantly over low heat until the cheese melts. Stir in the nutmeg and high-protein powder.

(NOTE: If you are using the whole clove of garlic, be sure to discard it before serving.)

Serves 3.

SPINACH NUT LOAF

1 package fresh spinach, washed
and cut fine
1 finely chopped onion
2 tablespoons chopped parsley
1 cup pignolias or blanched peanuts, ground fine

1 egg, well beaten
1 cup fine bread crumbs
cracker meal or wheat germ
vegetable oil
salt and pepper to taste

Steam the spinach, onion, and parsley in a waterless cooker for about 10 minutes, or until tender; add the nuts, egg, and bread brumbs, and mix together thoroughly. Shape into a loaf, brush with vegetable oil, and cover with Fay Lavan's Mix (see Index) or wheat germ. Bake for about 25 minutes in a preheated, moderate (350°F.) oven.

Serves 4.

SPINACH AND RICE

1 pound fresh spinach, washed
    and chopped
1 cup brown rice
¼ cup oil
2 fresh or 1 1-pound can toma-
    toes, chopped

1 medium-size onion, chopped
1 teaspoon mint (optional)
1 teaspoon vegetable salt

Brown the onion and rice in the oil. Add spinach, tomatoes,
onion, and seasoning; mix well together. Cover; simmer until
the rice is cooked (about 35 minutes), adding water as it is
needed.

Serves 6.

SWEET POTATO PIZZA

5 or 6 large sweet potatoes or
    yams
1 pound ground beef
1 medium-size onion, minced
2 tablespoons oil

2 teaspoons oregano
2 teaspoons sea salt
¼ teaspoon pepper
1 or 2 ripe tomatoes

Cook the sweet potatoes in slightly salted water until tender.
Drain, peel, and mash thoroughly, seasoning with 1 teaspoon
of the sea salt. Spread the mixture into an oiled 9-inch by
10-inch baking dish, patting it down firmly.

Heat the oil in a skillet and sauté the beef and onion
until the beef is lightly browned, then mix in thoroughly the
remaining sea salt, pepper, and oregano. Remove from heat.
Spread this mixture evenly on top of the sweet potatoes.

Immerse the tomatoes in boiling water and let them stay
there just long enough so the skins can be slipped off easily.
Slice them very thin or chop them fine; spread over the layer
of beef. Bake the "pizza" in a preheated oven at 350°F. for
30 minutes, or until the mixture is bubbly.

Serves 6 to 8.

BAKED STUFFED TOMATOES

6 medium-size tomatoes
⅓ cup peanut butter
¾ cup wheat germ
1 teaspoon sea salt
  pepper to taste

½ teaspoon oregano
1 tablespoon onion
¼ cup minced celery
  parsley for garnish

Scoop out pulp from tomatoes, reserving the shells; dice the pulp and drain, reserving the juice. Add the juice to the peanut butter, mixing it in well; mix in the remaining ingredients, but add the tomato pulp last. Fill the tomato shells with the mixture; place them in an oiled flat baking dish, and bake in a preheated oven at 400°F. for 25 to 30 minutes. Garnish with parsley before serving.

   Serves 6.

STUFFED SWEET POTATO

3 large sweet potatoes
1 cup fresh cranberries
¼ cup raisins
½ cup shelled walnuts

½ cup sesame seeds
1 teaspoon ground kelp
  butter or margarine as needed

Cook the sweet potatoes in their jackets just until tender. Cut each in half lengthwise and spoon out the centers; mash. Put the cranberries, raisins, walnuts, and sesame seed through a food chopper, then mix with the mashed potatoes. Add the kelp. Fill the potato skins with this mixture and dot generously with butter (or margarine). Place on a baking sheet and bake in a preheated oven at 350°F. for 30 minutes.

   Serves 6.

ZUCCHINI CRISPS

1 zucchini (about 6 inches)   wheat germ
1 egg, beaten   sea salt and pepper to taste

Peel the zucchini; cut into ⅛-inch slices. Dip each slice first
into beaten egg, then into wheat germ. Place on an oiled
baking sheet, sprinkle with salt and pepper, and bake in a
preheated oven at 375°F. for 15 minutes or until crisp.

ZUCCHINI STEW

4 or 5 medium-size zucchini   3 tablespoons olive oil or cold-
1 pound fresh tomatoes   pressed oil
1 cup chopped onion or green   1 teaspoon ground kelp
   onions (stems and all)   1 teaspoon crushed basil, fresh
1 medium-size green bell pep-   or dried
   per, chopped

Scrub the zucchini well but do not remove the skins; slice.
Cut the tomatoes into chunks. Heat the oil in a cast-iron
skillet and sauté the onions until soft (for 1 or 2 minutes).
Add the zucchini, tomatoes, bell pepper, kelp, and basil, and
mix well. Cover the skillet tightly and let the mixture simmer
for about 15 minutes.

Serves 4.

Breads and Crackers

WHOLE WHEAT BREAD

2 cups milk
2 tablespoons soy or safflower
oil
1½ teaspoons sea salt
4 tablespoons honey

1 cake fresh yeast or 1 envelope
dried yeast
½ cup warm water
7 cups (approximately) whole
wheat flour

Scald the milk; add oil, salt, honey to it; let cool. Dissolve
the yeast in the warm water, then add to the scalded milk
mixture. Gradually beat in enough of the flour to make a
stiff dough. Turn out onto a generously floured board and
knead for about 12 minutes (or use dough hook of electric
mixer), working in as much of the balance of flour as the
dough will take up, until it is smooth and satiny. (Too little
kneading will make for a heavy loaf of bread.)

Place the dough in an oiled mixing bowl, turning the
dough so all surfaces are coated with oil; cover with a
clean cloth; let stand in a warm place, free from drafts, until
it is double in bulk (about 1 hour). Punch down in the
bowl; cover; let rise again until doubled in bulk. Punch
down again and place on the kneading board. Divide the
dough into two equal parts and shape each into a loaf. Place
the loaves in greased 9-inch loaf pans; cover; let stand in a
warm place until the dough rises to the top of the pans and
is approximately double in bulk. Bake in a preheated oven
at 375°F. for about 1 hour, or until the loaves are browned
and sound hollow when rapped. Turn out onto racks to cool.

For a crisper crust, you may brush the tops of the loaves
with butter while they are still hot.

143

BANANA NUT BREAD

2 cups whole wheat pastry flour
1 teaspoon salt
4 teaspoons baking powder
½ cup butter or margarine
1 cup raw sugar
3 eggs, beaten

4 ripe bananas, mashed
⅝ cup milk
1 teaspoon any flavoring (optional)
1 cup chopped walnuts or pecans

Sift the salt, baking powder, and flour together and set aside. Cream the butter or margarine and sugar together in a bowl until fluffy. Beat in the eggs and mashed bananas until the mixture is thoroughly blended. Add the flavoring, if you are using it (the bread has a more pronounced banana flavor if no additional flavoring is used). Add the sifted dry ingredients to the banana mixture alternately with the milk, blending in carefully. Fold in the nuts. Turn the batter into a greased 9-inch loaf pan and bake in a preheated oven at 350° F. for about 1 hour, or until a cake tester inserted in the middle comes out clean. Cool on a rack.

NUT BREAD

2 cups whole wheat pastry flour or unbleached white flour
3 teaspoons tartrate-type baking powder
1 teaspoon salt
½ cup dark brown sugar or raw sugar

¼ cup oil or melted butter
1 cup milk
2 eggs
1 teaspoon flavoring (vanilla, maple, almond, or lemon)
½ cup chopped walnuts

Sift flour, salt, and baking powder together in a large bowl; add sugar, oil, eggs, and milk. Beat thoroughly. Blend in nuts. Turn into a greased loaf pan, and let stand for 20 minutes. Bake in a preheated oven at 350°F. for about an hour, or until a cake tester inserted in the middle comes out clean. Cool before slicing.

PUMPKIN BREAD

3½ cups unbleached flour
½ teaspoon baking powder
2 teaspoons baking soda
1½ teaspoons salt
1½ cups blackstrap molasses
2 cups cooked, mashed pumpkin

4 eggs
1 cup oil
⅔ cup water
1 teaspoon each of cloves, nutmeg, and cinnamon

Sift the dry ingredients together into a large bowl, then add the rest of the ingredients. Beat thoroughly. Turn into 2 greased and floured loaf pans. Bake in a preheated oven at 325°F. for about 1 hour and 25 minutes, or until a cake tester inserted in the middle comes out clean. Turn out onto a rack to cool.

HEALTH MUFFINS

1 small can any low-calorie fruit
1 egg
2 tablespoons honey
½ teaspoon sea salt
2 teaspoons baking powder

1½ cups finely ground wheat-germ flour
½ cup seedless raisins
1 tablespoon rice flour

Put the first four ingredients into a blender and blend until fruit is pureed and ingredients are thoroughly blended. In a bowl, mix the baking powder well with the wheat-germ flour. Pour in contents of blender jar and mix thoroughly.

Stir raisins and rice flour so raisins are well coated and will not sink in the baking, and add to batter, mixing only enough to blend. Spoon batter into buttered muffin pans and bake in a preheated 375°F. oven for about 30 minutes.

Makes 18 small or 12 average-size muffins.

NOTE: These are also good served for dessert.

WHEAT-GERM MUFFINS

1 cup unbleached flour	1 teaspoon grated orange rind
½ teaspoon salt	1 cup milk
4 teaspoons baking powder	1 cup wheat germ
¼ cup margarine or butter	¼ cup raisins
¼ cup raw or brown sugar	¼ cup dates, chopped
1 egg, well beaten	

Sift, then measure flour; resift with salt and baking powder. Cream shortening and sugar until light; add egg and orange rind, blending in thoroughly. Mix in sifted dry ingredients alternately with milk, stiring only enough to blend. Do not overbeat. Finally, fold in wheat germ, raisins, and dates. Spoon into buttered muffin pans, half-filling them. Bake in a preheated 375°F. oven for 25 to 30 minutes or until well risen and lightly browned.

Makes 18 small or 12 average-size muffins.

GLUTEN SESAME THINS

1½ cups gluten mix*	6 tablespoons water
3 tablespoons oil	sesame seeds
½ teaspoon salt	coarse salt

Add the oil and ½ teaspoon salt to the gluten mix, then add the water. Work the whole together to form a firm ball. Divide this in half; set 1 piece aside. Roll out the remaining half into a rectangle and sprinkle generously with the sesame seeds, and continue to roll the dough, making it as thin as possible. Sprinkle with a little coarse salt. Lift the whole

---

*Can be purchased at a health-food store.

sheet of dough (use a wide spatula and work carefully) onto a baking sheet. Score the dough into diamonds, but do not cut all the way through. Prepare the remaining piece of dough the same way.

Bake in a preheated oven at 450°F. for 8 to 10 minutes or until brown. Place the baking sheets onto racks to cool. Separate the crackers after they are cool.

SPOON BREAD

4 cups milk	4 eggs, beaten
1 cup corn meal	4 tablespoons melted butter

Mix all the ingredients together only until blended, then pour into a buttered 2-quart casserole. Bake in a preheated 375°-F. oven for about 45 minutes.

Breakfast Dishes

Make breakfast delectable—make it a meal that will give your family a head start. Here are breakfast dishes that are festive enough to double as desserts, yet they are rich in rutin, niacin, and all the B vitamins.

Full of nutrients and a nice change for the morning menu are pancakes; high-protein omelets; oatmeal with applesauce, high-protein powder, cinnamon, and raisins; bran flakes with prunes and apricots topped with milk or yogurt. All make good eating to cure morning sluggishness!

PROTEIN ENERGY OMELET

Use these proportions for each serving.

2 eggs	garlic powder to taste
1 teaspoon soya powder	sea salt to taste
1 teaspoon chia seeds	3 teaspoons safflower oil
1 teaspoon sunflower seeds	honey (optional)
1 teaspoon sesame seeds	

Put all the seeds into a blender and chop coarsely for a few seconds. Beat the eggs in a bowl with the soya powder and add chopped, mixed seeds. Season with the garlic powder and salt, and mix well. Heat the oil in a pan, then pour in the egg mixture. Cook gently until set (until omelet begins to crisp at the sides), then turn and cook another minute or so. Turn out onto a plate and serve immediately, with honey, if you like.

NOTE: Keep a jar of the mixed seeds in the refrigerator and use as needed.

BARLEY PANCAKES

2 tablespoons honey	1 cup soy milk
½ cup warm water	2 tablespoons vegetable oil
2 eggs	1 cup wheat germ
1 cup barley flour	

Pour the water into a mixing bowl, add the honey; let stand for 30 minutes in a warm place. Add the rest of the ingredients and mix well. Bake on a moderately hot oiled griddle until golden brown on each side. Spread with cashew butter and top with honey. These are delicious as an accompaniment to soft-boiled eggs.

CEREALS

1 cup millet or oatmeal or buck-   pinch salt (optional)
    wheat groats   ⅓ cup skim milk powder
1 quart (approximately) water

Bring water to a boil in the top half of a double boiler, and
add salt. Sprinkle in the cereal, stirring all the while. Cook
gently over direct heat for a few minutes, stirring frequently, then continue cooking over water (in the double
boiler). Just before serving, add skim milk powder (mix it
in well). Serve with cinnamon, applesauce, raisins, or
coconut.

BUCKWHEAT DELIGHT

½ cup buckwheat groats   ½ cup raisins
2½ cups boiling water   ¼ cup chopped dates
    honey to taste   ¼ cup coconut

Stir the groats into the water; sweeten to taste with the
honey; add the raisins and dates. Cook for about 12 minutes,
stirring occasionally so it does not stick. When it is almost
cooked, stir in the coconut. This is delicious served hot or
cold.
    Serves 4.

BAKED BREAKFAST RICE

2 cups cooked brown rice   1¼ cups soy milk
1 cup raisins

Mix together all ingredients and pour into a deep buttered
casserole. Cover, and bake in a preheated oven for 45 minutes at 325°F. Serve hot with honey and additional soy milk.
    NOTE: This dish may be prepared the evening before it
is to be used and refrigerated overnight. Slip the casserole
into the oven on arising, and breakfast will be ready when
the family is.

ENERGY HOT CAKES

3 cups Soy-O Pancake Flour
3 eggs, beaten
2 cups buttermilk
2 cups water
¼ cup wheat germ, toasted

2 tablespoons peanut oil
   (skimmed from a jar of peanut butter)
¼ cup chia seeds
Bac-O-Chips

Beat eggs, oil, water, and buttermilk together in a bowl. Add the soy flour, and mix until fairly smooth. Mix in the wheat germ and chia seeds. Bake on an oiled, moderately hot griddle until golden brown on both sides.

Serves 6.

OAT-CORN CRUMBLES

2⅔ cups oatmeal
⅓ cup wheat germ
1 cup whole grain cornmeal
¾ teaspoon sea salt
1 tablespoon sunflower seed
   kernels

1 tablespoon sesame seeds
3 tablespoons oil
⅔ cup hot water
¼ cup coarsely shredded coconut

Mix together well the oatmeal, wheat germ, cornmeal, sea salt, and seeds. Place the oil and honey in a large bowl, add the hot water; mix well. Stir in coconut. Add the dry ingredients, mixing until the whole is well blended and crumbly. Turn into a large, oiled pan. Bake in a preheated oven at 350°F. for about 1½ hours, until brown and crisp. Stir occasionally while baking.

This can be served hot or cold, with milk and honey or blackstrap molasses (preferably Barbados).

CORN FRITTERS

6 ears corn
2 eggs

salt and pepper to taste
wheat germ (optional)

Slit the grains with a fork and scrape the corn from the cobs. Beat together thoroughly the eggs and corn, and blend in seasonings. If mixture seems too thin, add a little wheat germ, stirring it in well. Bake like griddle cakes on a moderately hot oiled griddle. Serve with honey or maple syrup.
Serves 6.

Sauces and Relishes

PICKLED MUSHROOMS

2 cups small whole or large cut-up mushrooms
1 teaspoon sea salt
1 bay leaf

1 clove garlic, minced
1 teaspoon fennel seed
cider vinegar as needed

Sprinkle mushrooms with sea salt; set aside. Pour the vinegar into a saucepan (start with 1 cup; you will need enough to cover the mushrooms), add the garlic, bay leaf, and fennel, and heat to simmering. Add the mushrooms; simmer for 5 minutes. Pour into hot sterilized jars; seal.
Makes about 1 pint. This is good to serve with meat instead of relish or pickles.

MOCK HOLLANDAISE SAUCE

1 cup diced potatoes
¼ cup diced carrots
¾ cup water

1 tablespoon vegetable oil
½ teaspoon sea salt
1 tablespoon cider vinegar

Cook the potatoes and carrots in the water until tender (about 20 minutes). Turn into a blender and puree. Add the rest of the ingredients and blend until smooth.
Serve with broccoli or asparagus.

SOY MAYONNAISE

¾ cup water	¼ cup lemon juice
¾ cup soya bean powder	1 cup vegetable oil
½ teaspoon sea salt	

Stir the soya bean powder into the oil, then slowly add the other ingredients to the mixture, stirring continuously until well blended.

Makes about 1 pint.

CRANBERRY-APPLE RELISH

1 pound fresh cranberries	2 cups pineapple juice or apple juice
5 pounds apples (mixed McIntosh, Cortland, yellow Delicious, or such)	1 teaspoon cinnamon

Pare and slice the apples; place in a large kettle with the washed and picked-over cranberries; add the juice. Simmer for about 1½ hours. Add cinnamon; cook for another 30 minutes.

NOTE: This relish keeps well for several weeks under refrigeration.

COCKTAIL SAUCE

¾ cup catsup	1 tablespoon Worcestershire sauce
2 to 4 tablespoons freshly grated horseradish or ¼ cup prepared horseradish	2 tablespoons lemon juice
10 drops Tabasco sauce	¼ teaspoon salt

Mix all ingredients well together. Serve with shrimp, oysters, crab meat, or other seafood.

Makes about 1 cup.

SAUCE FOR CHICKEN, LAMB, OR PORK

1 pound ripe tomatoes, chopped
2 whole cloves of garlic
2 medium-size oranges, unpeeled,
    sliced thin, and seeded

sea salt to taste
1 teaspoon raw honey
   cold-pressed oil as needed
¼ cup (approximately)

Sauté the garlic in oil for several minutes, then add the chopped tomatoes, salt, and honey. Cook for about 10 minutes over medium heat. Add the orange slices. Simmer slowly, uncovered, for about 20 minutes more. Unless you have a particular passion for garlic, remove the cloves before serving.

Desserts and Snacks

Included in this section are desserts that are delicious and festive enough for company yet simple enough for a family affair: great desserts that taste immoral, illegal, and fattening—but aren't.

PRUNE GELATIN

1 pound large prunes
1 quart boiling water

2½ tablespoons gelatin
1 cup cold water

Pour boiling water over the prunes and let them stand overnight to plump up. In the morning, soften the gelatin in cold water. Heat the water in which the prunes soaked; pour it over the softened gelatin; stir until dissolved. Pit the prunes. Put half of them in a blender with half the gelatin mixture until completely blended and pureed. Repeat with the rest of the prunes and gelatin. Mix the two batches together, and pour into a mold. Refrigerate for several hours, until firm. Unmold to serve.

    Serves 8.

HONEY SPREAD

1 cup wheat germ   2 cups pumpkin-seed meal
1 cup sunflower-seed meal   2 cups honey

Put all the dry ingredients into a wide-mouthed jar (like a mason jar) and shake well so they are evenly distributed. Add the honey, cutting it in with a knife (or screw the cap on the jar and then turn the jar a sufficient number of times) so the honey is absorbed thoroughly and uniformly by the dry ingredients.

Serve with apple slices.

PINEAPPLE NUT TORTE

5 large eggs, separated   1½ cups wheat germ
½ cup raw honey   1 20-ounce can unsweetened
3 cups ground walnuts or   crushed pineapple, drained
   pecans

Beat egg yolks until light; add honey, and beat again until thoroughly blended. Beat in wheat germ and nuts. Add crushed pineapple, stirring in well. Fold in stiffly beaten egg whites. Bake in a preheated oven in 2 greased 9-inch cake pans or 1 large greased spring-form pan for about 30 minutes at 325°F.

ORANGE SOUP

2 cups unsweetened orange juice   3 tablespoons cold water
2 teaspoons cornstarch or arrow-   honey to sweeten
   root starch

Heat juice in saucepan. Mix cornstarch (or arrowroot starch) with cold water until smooth, then add to the hot juice. Cook slowly, stirring constantly, until mixture is clear. Add honey to taste. Chill. Serve ice cold, as a dessert, in frosted sherbet glasses. (To frost glasses, place in freezer until ready to use.)

Serves 2 or 3.

Variations

Prepare as above, substituting other juices or a combination of juices for the orange juice.

UNBAKED COCONUT CHEESE CAKE

1 tablespoon unflavored gelatin
¼ cup cold water
¼ cup hot water
2 teaspoons grated lemon rind
1 tablespoon honey

2 cups cream-style cottage cheese
1 cup unsweetened pineapple juice
freshly grated coconut

Stir gelatin into cold water to soften, then dissolve in hot water. Add lemon rind, honey, and pineapple juice; mix well. Fold in cottage cheese that has been whipped to a creamy consistency (use a blender or electric mixer for this). Oil a 9-inch glass pie plate. Press a layer of the coconut onto the bottom and sides. Pour in the cheese mixture; sprinkle generously with additional coconut. Chill.

Serves 6.

APPLE CAKE

1 cup whole wheat pastry flour
¼ teaspoon salt
1 teaspoon baking soda
1 teaspoon cinnamon
1 cup dark brown sugar, firmly packed

1 egg, beaten
¼ cup oil
2 cups raw, diced apples (unsprayed)
1 cup chopped nuts

Sift together flour, salt, soda, and cinnamon. Place sugar and egg in a bowl, beat thoroughly; add oil; beat until thick and light. Stir in sifted dry ingredients, then stir in apples (if the batter appears too thick, add a very small amount of apple juice). Fold in the nuts, after reserving a couple of spoonfuls; sprinkle those over the top of the cake. Bake in a preheated oven in a large oiled and floured pan (or in two 8 × 8-inch pans) for about 35 minutes at 350°F., or until a straw inserted in the cake comes out dry.

RHUBARB CUSTARD

1 pound rhubarb, cut into 1-inch lengths	¼ cup sugar
	½ cup honey
3 eggs, separated	1 cup milk

Put egg yolks, honey and milk into a blender and blend well. Put rhubarb pieces into a baking dish and pour the egg mixture over it. Beat the egg whites and sugar together until very stiff (to make a meringue) and spoon onto the custard mixture. Place this pan in a larger pan of hot water and bake in the lower half of a preheated oven at 375°F. for about 40 minutes, or until a knife inserted in the center comes out clean.

SOYBEAN SNACKS

¼ cup dried soybeans	1 cup cold water
oil as needed (optional)	seasoning to taste (optional)

Soak soybeans, with water to cover, overnight in the refrigerator. Next day, drain the liquid, reserving it as stock. Dry the soybeans on a clean towel, then spread them in a shallow pan. Roast in the oven for 2 hours at 200°F., then place under broiler, stirring the soybeans frequently, until they are brown.

The beans may be eaten as is, or oiled and seasoned. Or use as a topping in the same way as you would nuts, either whole, or ground in a blender or food grinder.

Part Three

NUTRITIONAL SUPPLEMENTS

Diet, Health, and Vitamins

Scientists and nutrition researchers are penetrating deeper into the relationship between food and disease, and they continue to discover new, previously unknown elements, such as vitamins B_{15} and B_{17}, in our foods. One initial stride toward improved health was made in 1912 by Dr. Casimir Funk, who discovered in rice polishings the substance that could cure beriberi, and who coined the term "vitamine."

There are many fascinating stories about nutrition. For instance, once it was learned that scurvy (a dread affliction of men who sailed the seas and one that was caused by a lack of vitamin C) could be prevented by giving sailors limes, British sailors were given these daily, for "a lime a day keeps scurvy away." And so British sailors today are referred to as "limeys."

Vitamins may be regarded as accessory food factors, organic in origin and required for normal, healthy function of the body. Their absence leads to the so-called deficiency diseases. About fifteen substances can definitely be classed as vitamins; there are another fifteen that may be vitamins, and it is probable that many other vitamins will be discovered.

TYPES OF VITAMINS

Many vitamins are destroyed by exposure to light, air, heat, improper cooking, or storage. They can be also destroyed when the acid-alkaline balance in the body is off, and they can be absorbed only in the presence of sufficient hydrochloric acid.

Vitamin A is a fat-soluble vitamin. It is found in fish (one good source is cod liver oil), liver, eggs, and dairy foods. It is present as well in some vegetables (in particular, in carrots; the provitamin carotene is converted in the liver to vitamin A) and in fruits. For those who cannot tolerate oils, water-soluble vitamin A is available.

*Vitamin B₁—thiamine—*is important in carbohydrate metabolism. It increases energy and mental alertness; it alleviates digestive disturbances and constipation.

Vitamin B₂—riboflavin, also known as *vitamin G—*is part of the B-complex group and works together with vitamin A. Its enzymatic action helps the eyes function better.

*Vitamin B₃—niacin—*is also part of the B-complex group. Much research is being done on B₃ in relation to schizophrenia.

*Vitamin B₆—pyridoxine—*is important in protein and fat metabolism. It is also particularly helpful in cases of edema of the hands and to alleviate leg cramps.

*Vitamin B₁₂—cyanocobalamin—*is given for anemia. It is excellent also to use in cases of postoperative and general convalescence, giving the patient a much-needed quick "lift."

*Vitamin C—ascorbic acid—*is found in acerola, rose hips, citrus fruits, and tomatoes. It is important in fighting infections such as the common cold, sore gums, and skin problems.

Vitamin D, frequently called the "sunshine vitamin," is probably best known for its curative effects on rickets. It is also helpful in healing bones. It is generally taken in conjunction with vitamin A.

*Vitamin E—*any of the *tocopherols—*is a natural constituent of the body that prevents destruction of adrenal and sex hormones, and is also helpful in dissolving blood clots associated with varicose veins and phlebitis. It is found in wheat-germ oil.

Vitamin G. See Vitamin B₂

*Vitamin H—biotin—*is another member of the B-complex group. It is helpful in relieving eczema and in combating loss of hair. The richest source is yeast.

Vitamin K, a fat-soluble compound, is the "blood-clotting vitamin."

*Vitamin P—bioflavonoid—*strengthens the capillaries and blood vessels of the outer extremities. *Hesperidin* is found in most citrus fruits, especially in the peel of oranges; *rutin* (vitamin P_4) is found in buckwheat groats and eucalyptus.

Vitamin T, helpful in the improvement of memory, comes from sesame-seed oil.

Ascorbic acid. See *Vitamin C.*

Choline is a member of the B-complex group. It is helpful in lowering cholesterol. The best sources for this are lecithin and soy products.

Folic acid, another member of the B-complex group, is important in growth. A deficiency can lead to loss of appetite or even anemia. It is found in liver and other organ meats and in whole grains.

Hesperidin. See *Vitamin P.*

Inositol, also in the B-complex group, is an essential factor in growth and a lipotropic factor concerned with fat. It affects the skin, appetite, and cholesterol. Lecithin is one source.

Pantothenic acid is a member of the B-complex group that is helpful in reducing uric acid and is essential for cell growth. It is found in sweetbreads, brains, liver, tongue and lungs, and also in yeast, egg yolks, peanuts, rice bran, broccoli, salmon, and soybeans.

Para-aminobenzoic acid, a member of the B-complex group, is used in restoring skin and hair color.

Rutin. See *Vitamin P.*

Minerals and Nutrients

The body needs at least sixteen minerals to sustain energy and extend life. They are necessary to nourish the blood, bones, brain, hair, heart, nerves, and teeth, and are important for the proper functioning of all glands. They work together with vitamins.

The most important and familiar minerals are: calcium, iron, magnesium, phosphorus, and potassium. Also important are the many so-called trace elements or minerals. A deficiency of any one or more of these minerals may be responsible for an unexplained illness or even just a feeling of malaise, as experienced and described by some of the writers of the letters in Part One.

Calcium, especially needed for healthy bones and teeth, is most easily obtained from milk products. Those allergic to milk can obtain calcium from bone meal (either in powder or tablet form), or from calcium lactate or calcium gluconate.

Iron is important to the functioning of the entire body. It is needed for the formation of red corpuscles, tissue respiration, and carrying oxygen in the blood. A lack of iron is one of the causes of anemia. Foods that are important sources of iron are soybeans, lima beans, peas, blackstrap molasses, egg yolks, lean beef, liver, oatmeal, and dried fruits.

Magnesium helps maintain tissue excitability and prevents constipation. It is available in tablet or powder form and, in its natural state, in most foods grown in rich soil, but they must not be boiled or soaked before serving.

Phosphorus is needed for the liver and growing tissue, and is as important as protein for body building.

Potassium prevents muscle stiffness and prolongs agility in middle-aged and older persons.

TRACE MINERALS

Trace minerals found in many tissues, but not yet known to have any special function, are *aluminum, arsenic, nickel,* and *silicon.*

Iodine is a constituent of the hormone thyroxine, which controls the body's metabolic rate, and is vital for proper functioning of the thyroid gland. It can be obtained from seafood (fish and shellfish), kelp, and iodized salt. For a good supply, eat seafood twice weekly. Radishes, watercress, lemon, egg yolk, garlic, and onions are also rich in iodine.

Copper helps the body make use of iron. A deficiency leads to anemia, since the body cannot make use of iron without copper.

Sulfur occurs in the protein of tissues and can be obtained from all vegetables grown in properly composted soil.

Sodium is needed in moderation in body fluids, but its intake should be kept to a minimum in cases of high blood pressure.

Chlorine is important in forming hydrochloric acid in the stomach. It is found in green leafy vegetables and in table salt.

Manganese is an enzymes activator and aids in utilizing fats. The best sources for this are wheat germ, bran, leafy vegetables, and whole grains.

Cobalt is a constituent of vitamin B_{12}. Without it, anemia results. Sore tongue is sometimes evidence of a cobalt deficiency. Best sources are meat, eggs, fruit, vegetables.

Molybdenum is an activator of the enzyme systems, and is considered an essential element.

Chromium is essential; it is needed before the body can utilize sugar.

Flourine, in combination with calcium phosphorus, is closely concerned with bones and teeth formation.

Zinc is needed for proper growth of hair and for the proper function of insulin in carbohydrate metabolism. It abounds in nuts, fruits, and vegetables grown in rich soil.

Recommended Foods

Food is the material that nourishes, sustains, and supports the body. The food that enters your system must be assimilated by it and contribute to its life, growth, and power for work.

The foods listed below are among those that best help the body grow and work:

Acerola and *rose hips* are the best sources for vitamin C. They are available in powder or tablet form, or as tea.

Acidophilus milk. See *Yogurt, acidophilus milk, and buttermilk.*

Basil (about 1 teaspoonful of the ground herb dissolved in a pan of water) can be used to soak the chemical residue from fruits and vegetables that have been sprayed.

Beans. See *Lentils.*

Blackstrap molasses, which is both a natural food and a remedy, contains vitamin B complex, vitamin B_6, and inositol.

Bone meal, calcium lactate, and *calcium gluconate* are sources of calcium. They come in powder or tablet form and are recommended for bone healing and general health, and especially as a preventative for osteoporosis.

Brewers' yeast is a unique and concentrated natural food

of the B-complex family. In powder form, it can be added to juice or other foods. It is also available in tablets.

Buckwheat groats, which contain rutin and magnesium, are an excellent food to use in place of potatoes or rice.

Buttermilk. See *Yogurt, acidophilus milk, and buttermilk.*

Carob, also known as *St. John's bread,* can be used as a substitute for chocolate.

Cheeses (*unprocessed*) are a good source of calcium and protein.

Desiccated liver is a rich source of protein and vitamin B complex. It is made from whole liver dried at low temperature to preserve the nutrients. It is best taken mixed in vegetable juice. See also *Liver.*

Eggs and *egg yolks* are rich in biotin, choline, and vitamins B_3 and D.

Fennel seeds, when chewed thoroughly, relieve nasal congestion.

Fish liver oil contains vitamin A and comes primarily from cod, halibut, and shark.

Fruits should be included in the diet at least twice daily for their vitamin C content (all fruits contain vitamin C in varying amounts). *Fresh fruits* are one of nature's natural cleansers. *Dried and unsulfured fruits* (apricots, raisins, etc.), when combined with unsalted roasted nuts, make an excellent snack.

Groats. See *Buckwheat groats.*

Heart and *kidney* contain vitamins B_6, B_3, and B_1.

Herbs are medicine from the meadows. They add zest to the health way of life.

High-protein powder should be used to enrich milk drinks and soups, particularly for the elderly and underweight.

Honey (*unpasteurized*) is nature's elixir for health and energy. Use in place of white sugar.

Horseradish can be used in place of salt. It is recommended for weak vision, anemia, stiff muscles, and loss of energy.

Juices (raw) such as apple, carrot, celery, and grape, freshly prepared, are therapeutic. A juice machine constitutes a good investment for health.

Kelp (seaweed), dried, is rich in iodine, potassium, phosphorus, and other mineral salts. It is black in color. It can be purchased as a powder or in tablet form, and can be used in place of table salt. See also *Sea Salt.*

Kidney. See *Heart and kidney.*

Lactose (milk sugar) digests easily. Noninstant-type powdered skim milk contains 56 percent lactose; powdered whey contains 95 percent lactose and must be taken with fat.

Lecithin, a soybean derivative, is believed to aid in lowering cholesterol, and is also helpful, in cases of arthritis, for relieving stiffness and pain. Use 3 tablespoons daily in cereal, juice, or soup.

Lemon and *orange peel,* grated or powdered, are excellent for seasoning.

Lentils, peas, and *beans* are rich in vitamin B_1.

Linseed oil. See *Oils.*

Liver contains biotin, choline, inositol, and vitamins B_6, B_3, and B complex. See also *Desiccated liver.*

Milk is a good source of vitamin D and calcium.

Milk sugar. See *Lactose.*

Muscle meats contain vitamin B_3.

Nuts are rich in vitamins B_3, B_1, and B_6.

Oatmeal and other cereals should be served enriched with high-protein or skim-milk powder.

Oils—safflower, sunflower, linseed, and *walnut*—contain essential fatty acids. Take 2 tablespoonsful daily in salad or other food.

Peas. See *Lentils.*

Potatoes (*white* and *sweet*) are rich in protein.

Rice—brown, wild, or *long grain,* and *not processed*—are all good. Use in place of ordinary white rice.

Rice polishings are a source of vitamin B₁.

Rose hips. See *Acerola and rose hips.*

Safflower oil. See *Oils.*

St. John's bread. See *Carob.*

Sea salt is dried salt from the sea. Rich in minerals, it can be used in place of table salt, but keep to a minimum. See also *Kelp.*

Seafood (*fish* and *shellfish*) is an important source of iodine. It should be eaten at least twice a week, but can be eaten as often as you wish. Fish is especially good for persons with a high cholesterol count.

Seeds and *seed meals,* such as pumpkin, sunflower, and sesame, contain vitamin B complex and vitamin D. Add them to your favorite recipes.

Soybean flour contains very little oil and is both palatable and nutritious. It makes excellent bread for diabetics.

Soybeans, containing vitamin B₁ and choline, are a wonder source of energy. Rivaling wheat in nutrition, they are also one of the great protein foods, for they contain two and a half times as much protein as meat. In addition, they are rich in thiamine (vitamin B₁), niacin (vitamin B₃), riboflavin (vitamin B₂), calcium, phosphorus, choline, and iron. The soybean is so interesting that it has merited special cookbooks (see your library for these).

Sprouted seeds and *whole grains* are excellent for a nutritious diet. Use them in salads and omelets, and add to main courses. There are a number of ways to sprout seeds. You can get directions for sprouting them from a health-food store, when you buy your grains, or you can follow the simple method explained below. You can sprout chick-peas, chia seeds, corn, barley, fenugreek, wheat, fresh yellow or green peas, lentils, oats, millet, sunflower seeds, and sesame seeds. Your health-food store can probably recommend other types of sprouters.

TO SPROUT SEEDS

Half fill a jar with tepid water. To this, add about 1 tablespoon of any of the seeds listed above. Let stand overnight, then rinse with lukewarm water. Cover the jar with a cloth and place in a cool, dark area (do not set in the refrigerator; that's too cold). Rinse the seeds at least twice a day with fresh water, being sure to keep them separated.

Sunflower oil. See *Oils.*

Vegetables (*green and leafy*) used in salads, are among nature's natural cleansers, and are sources of vitamins A, C, K, and choline. Use as many raw vegetables as possible, and try to eat salad twice daily. Cooked vegetables should be lightly steamed in a stainless steel pot.

Walnut oil. See *Oil.*

Wheat germ (*raw*) is a rich natural source of vitamins B_1, B_6, E, B complex, and choline. It can be sprinkled on cereals or used in place of bread crumbs wherever the latter are called for. Two tablespoons give you 16 grams of protein.

Whole grains—whole wheat, wheat germ, soya protein— should be used instead of white-flour products unless you have a wheat allergy. Be adventuresome and try the different breads made from these products. See also *Sprouted seeds.*

Yogurt, acidophilus milk, and *buttermilk* contain vitamin B complex. These fermented milks help to improve the intestinal flora.

Diet Supplements for Specific Problems

Not only the letters in Part One but also hundreds of articles and books relating to nutrition and vitamin therapy attest to the fact that certain foods and vitamins appear to be helpful in overcoming, alleviating—or even curing—particular conditions of ill health. Conversely, their lack can be responsible for some illnesses or problems. For instance, it is now common knowledge that beriberi is caused by a lack of the B vitamin, and rickets by a lack of vitamin D.

The list that follows matches helpful vitamins, minerals, and supplements to the organs in the body or the complaints or illnesses that are benefited by the regular intake of these dietary supplements.

THE PROBLEM	THE AIDS
Acne	A (easily obtained in carrots); E
Adrenals	C; pantothenic acid
Alcoholism	B complex; C
Allergies	C
Anemia	B_{12} H (biotin); folic acid; iron
Appetite (lack of)	B complex
Arteries	B; C; E
Arteriosclerosis	B_6; C; E; calcium
Asthma	A; E; para-aminobenzoic acid
Backache	C; D; E; dolomite; protein
Baldness	A; B_2; inositol
Beriberi	B complex; B_1
Bladder	A; D
control	B_6
Blood cells	folic acid
Blood clotting	C; D; E; K
Blood pressure	
high	C; E
low	C; pantothenic acid; protein
Blood vessels	A; B; B_2; C; D; E; choline

THE PROBLEM	THE AIDS
Bone marrow	B; C
Bones	
brittle	A; protein
healing	C; D; calcium
Brain	B; B$_2$; E
Breath (shortness of)	B complex
Bruising (*see also* Healing)	C
Burns	C; E
Bursitis	C; potassium
Cataracts	B; B$_2$; C; E
Cholesterol	C; F; choline; inositol; lecithin
Circulation	E
Colds	A; C; P
Colitis	B complex; C
Concentration (lack of)	B$_6$; sesame seeds (for vitamin P)
Conjunctivitis	B$_2$
Constipation	B complex; B$_1$; inositol; magnesium oxide
Coronary (*see also* Heart)	choline; inositol
Deafness	A; B; C
Depression	B$_3$ (niacin); B$_6$
Dermatitis	B$_6$; H (biotin); para-aminobenzoic acid
Diabetes	B$_6$; B$_{12}$; E; zinc
Diarrhea	B complex; B$_3$; C
Digestion	all B vitamins
Dizziness	B; protein
Ears	A
inner	B; C; E; P; garlic perles; potassium
tinnitus (ringing)	A; B complex
Ménière's disease	C
Eczema	B complex; B$_6$; H (biotin); para-aminobenzoic acid
Edema	B$_6$
Energy (lack of)	B$_1$
Epilepsy	B$_6$; B$_{12}$
Eyes	A; B complex; B$_1$; B$_2$; B$_6$; B$_{12}$; C; E; inositol; sunflower seeds
Fatigue	B complex

The Problem	The Aids
Feet (burning, restlessness)	B complex; B₂ (riboflavin); B₆
Flu	C
Gallbladder	A; K
Gas	B complex; B₆
Gastrointestinal tract	A; B; B₂; C
Glands	choline
Glaucoma	C
Gout	C; pantothenic acid
Gums	A; B complex; B₂; C; D; P
Hair (loss of and loss of color of)	B₂; H; para-aminobenzoic acid
Halitosis	B₆
Headache	B complex
Healing of bones	C; D; calcium
of wounds	C
Heart	A; B₁; E; H; choline, inositol
Hemorrhoids	B₆
Hypoglycemia	all-vitamin therapy; blueberry tea
Infections (viral)	C
Indigestion	B complex
Insect bites	A; E
Insomnia	B complex; calcium
Intervertebral disk	C
Irritability	B₆
Joints	C; F; P
Kidney(s)	A; D
stones	A; B₆; C; choline
Legs (cramps, numbness, restlessness)	B₆; C; D; E; calcium
Lethargy	B₆
Lips (dry, chapped, lined, puckered from age)	B₂
Liver	A; B; C
Lungs	A; B; B₁; C; D; H; para-aminobenzoic acid
Mammary glands	A; B
Memory (loss of)	B complex; sesame seeds

The Problem	The Aids
Menopause	E; wheat-germ oil; zinc
Menstrual disorders	C; E
Mental illness	
(*see also* Schizophrenia)	B_1; B_3 (niacin); C; E
Metabolism	B_1 choline
Muscle(s)	A; B; B_2; C; D; E
strain	B complex; B_6; C; E; P (bioflavinoid)
Muscular dystrophy	B_{12}; E
Nausea	B complex
Nerves	A; B; B complex; B_2 (G); B_6; C; D; E
Neuritis	B complex; B_1
Night blindness	A
Nose (-bleed; dryness)	A; C
Pancreas	B
Parathyroid	D; calcium
Pellagra	B complex; E
Phlebitis	E
Pituitary	B; E
Pleurisy	C
Prostate	A; E; F; pumpkin seeds (for linoleic acid and zinc)
Psoriasis	E
Respiratory ailments	A; C; E
Rheumatic fever	C
Rheumatism	A; B_{12}; C; D; E; brewers' yeast
Sexual organs	A; B; C; E
Scar tissue	E
Schizophrenia	B_3 (niacin); B_{12}
Sinus	A; C
Skin	A; B; B_2; C
abrasions	C; E; P (bioflavinoid)
disorders (*see also* Psoriasis, Vitiligo)	B complex; B_2; B_3; H; C
Spleen	B
Stomach cramps	B_6
Stress	C
Stroke	E; C

The Problem	The Aids
Teeth	C; calcium
Thymus	B
Thyroid	A; B; C; D; F
Tongue (soreness of)	A; B complex; B_2; B_6; B_{12}
Tonsillitis (or sore throat)	C
Ulcers	B_{12}; C; P (bioflavinoid); P_1
Varicose veins	C; E; P; pectin
Vitiligo	C; hydrochloric acid; para-aminobenzoic acid
Warts	E
Wound healing	C

FOLKLORE IN FOODS, NUTRITION, AND HEALTH REMEDIES

Folklore (or the traditional beliefs, legends, and customs of people) has often included a belief in the benefits derived from the use of herbs, flowers, and vegetables in the healing arts. These took the place of traditional medicines, which ofttimes were not available. Many of these old remedies have been carried over to the present. With the advent of the new and widening interest in natural foods, we have included here a few of those that in the past have been used as remedies and are harmless.

Almond oil: for fever and cosmetics.

Apple cider vinegar: 1 teaspoon in an 8-ounce glass of water for indigestion, as nasal douche, as ear douche.

Apricots, fresh: Seeds eaten ground very fine or squeezed to produce an oil that can be used for glossy hair, body bruises, as a tonic for circulation, for heart problems, to prevent wrinkles, for anemia.

Asparagus: anemia; as a sedative for the heart; for diabetics. Helpful for urine and nasal catarrah; as soup for rheumatic complaints; use the water from asparagus for joint pains.

Avocado: for the skin—rich in minerals and vitamins.

Bananas, Ripe: contain strong enzymes and help digestion and the assimilation of other foods

Basil: for sterility and sex; as a digestive for fish and rich foods; for fevers from kidney and bladder.

Beets: for influenza and uric acid; for arthritic, cardiac and circulatory complaints; for rheumatism.

Black Pepper: a gastrointestinal stimulant; for flatulence and indigestion.

Chervil, fresh: make juice for blood clots, kidney stones, urinary problems, pleurisy, gas and wind, ulcers.

Chives: Use as soup for rheumatic complaints; helpful for urine and nasal catarrh.

Cinnamon: antihemorrhage for nosebleeds.

Cucumber: for sunburn and freckles; firms the skin.

Garlic juice: mix with honey for asthma.

Leeks: for eyes, nasal catarrah, skin eruptions.

Magnesium oxide: for constipation.

Marjoram: a sexual nerve tonic; use in soup and milk

Nutmeg: for dizziness, flatulence, diarrhea; for dry mucus membranes.

Paprika: high in vitamin C.

Peas: contain chlorophyll, phosphate sulphur, potassium, magnesium; use for varicose veins, piles, and urinary complaints.

Rosemary: use for improvement of memory, as a brain tonic; use to restore speech after strokes; use for vertigo; for hair tonic.

Sage: as a gargle for relaxed throat; for quinsy, laryngitis, tonsils, mouth ulcers, and general health.

Sex foods: Parmesan cheese, fish, oysters, crabs, caviar, mushrooms.

Tarragon: for stings and bites; a sex and brain tonic.

Thyme: for strength and courage.

Watercress: for strength; removes kidney stones and gravel.

Food Values

PROTEIN

Nutritionists suggest that half the daily protein consumption should be from meat (with emphasis on liver and organ meats), milk, cheese, and eggs. One-half gram of protein is needed for every pound of body weight. Thus, if you weigh 120 pounds, you need 60 grams or more of protein daily.

When the diet is lacking in protein, the body cannot form sufficient albumin and waste material is not completely removed from the tissues. Still, there may be weeks or months of mild protein deficiency before the accumulated fluid in the body becomes noticeable. Instead of taking diuretics to get rid of the excess fluid, increase the intake of protein, and water loss should occur naturally.

This is how some of the more common foods compare in weight:

Milk: 1 cup = 8 gr.	Organ meats: 4 oz. = 20 gr.
Buttermilk: 1 cup = 8 gr.	Liver: 4 oz. = 20 gr.
Cottage cheese: ½ cup = 20 gr.	Fish: 4 oz. = 20 gr.
Eggs: 1 = 7 gr.	Fowl: 4 oz. = 23 gr.
Meat: 4 oz. = 20 gr.	Wheat germ: 1 tbsp. = 8 gr.

VEGETABLES

You may find that you do not use, often enough, those vegetables that are richest in the most-needed minerals. Do not serve only peas, carrots, potatoes, string beans, or asparagus; ues kale for calcium, leafy greens for chlorine, dried beans for copper, cabbage and onions for iodine, parsley for iron, kohlrabi for magnesium. Serve a new vegetable every day with one that is already familiar to you. Use a variety of greens, all dark—escarole, chicory, romaine—in your salads, as well as raw zucchini, celery, and fresh spinach leaves, for variety and for additional minerals and health.

The following vegetables supply vitamins A and K. Try to use several daily from this group.

Asparagus	Celery	Lettuce
Beans (dried)	Chard	Onions
Broccoli	Corn	Parsley
Brussel sprouts	Endive	Spinach
Cabbage	Green Peas	Squash
Carrots	Green Peppers	String beans
Cauliflower	Kale	Tomatoes
		Watercress

FRUITS AND FRUIT JUICES

As has been mentioned earlier, fruits are nature's laxatives, and nature has given us a wide variety from which to choose. (Nonetheless, most persons refuse to widen their taste horizons, and so they fail to partake sufficiently of nature's bounty.) It is the alkaline elements in fruit that combine with fruit acids to act as natural laxatives, and the bulk in the fruit is needed for the action of the bowels. The skin of fruits should be eaten whenever possible, but it should be masticated thoroughly because of the cellulose in it. In citrus fruits, the white part next to the skin contains vitamin K and bioflavonoids (vitamin P)—both important to good health.

The liquid in fruit removes impurities from the body. Persons who travel and are uncertain of the water in areas where they stay can safely use fruit juice in place of water. Fruit eaters need less water than noneaters of fruit. Persons who suffer from pruritis ani—itching of the rectum or the area between the buttocks, often caused by orange juice—may find that although they cannot drink orange juice, they can eat the whole fruit without a pruritic reaction.

Except for honey, the purest and most digestible forms of sweetening for adults and children are grape sugar and fruit sugar. Dried fruits are an excellent substitute for candy, especially for children.

Minerals and vitamin C are supplied by these fruits and juices. Take at least two of them daily.

Apples	Figs	Pineapples
Apricots	Grapefruit	Prunes
Bananas	Grapes	Raisins
Cherries	Melons (all kinds)	Strawberries or other
Cranberries or	Oranges	berries
cranberry juice	Peaches	Tomato juice
Dates	Pears	

NUTS

These nuts have the highest protein value and are lowest in calories, according to the *Agricultural Handbook #8* (published by the U.S. Department of Agriculture). Try to eat 2 ounces daily.

Almonds	Peanuts	Pistachios
Cashews	Pecans	

WHOLE GRAINS AND SUPPLEMENTS

Do you know what is meant by "whole-grain," "restored," and "enriched," when referring to cereals? A "whole-grain" cereal contains all three principal parts of the cereal—the inner germ, the endosperm, and the outer layer of bran. Whole wheat and oats are examples of whole-grain cereals. During the milling process, the principal nutrients are lost; cereals in which they are replaced are known as "restored" cereals. Cereal products are referred to as "enriched" when thiamine (vitamin B_1), riboflavin (vitamin B_2,), niacin (vitamin B_3), and some iron have been added to them.

All of the following help prevent deficiencies of the B vitamins, vitamin E, and iron.

Bone meal	Buckwheat groats	Sweet Potatoes
Brewers' yeast	(kasha)	Wheat Germ
Brown rice	Lecithin	White potatoes
		Whole-grain bread

Shopping List

With these ingredients in your larder, you can enjoy an endless variety of dishes—all nutritious and all delicious. Do not, however, limit yourself to these; this is not a complete list, but merely a basic one, including ingredients too frequently omitted. With these on hand you are always ready to make bread or prepare desserts.

BEVERAGES	CEREALS	FLOURS
Apple juice	Brown Rice	Peanut
Cranberry juice	Buckwheat groats	Rice
Grape juice	(kasha)	Soy
Grapefruit juice	Brown Rice	Wheat-germ
Orange juice	Grits	Whole-wheat
Pineapple juice	Oatmeal	Whole-wheat-pastry
	Wheat germ	

FRUITS (FRESH)	FRUITS (DRIED AND UNSULFURED)	NUTS AND SEEDS
Apples	Cranberries	Almonds
Apricots	Dates	Cashews
Avocados	Figs	Coconut
Berries in season	Prunes	Corn (for popcorn)
Melons (all kinds)	Raisins	Peanuts
Peaches		Pecans
Pears		Pumpkin Seeds
Pineapples		Sunflower Seeds
Strawberries		Sesame Seeds
		Walnuts

OILS	SEASONINGS	SWEETENERS
Corn	Allspice	Blackstrap molasses
Safflower	Carob powder	Date sugar
Sesame	Cinnamon	Honey
Soy	Cloves	Maple syrup
Sunflower	Ginger	Raw sugar
	Kelp, ground	
	Lemon rind, grated	
	Orange rind, grated	
	Vanilla	

MISCELLANEOUS

Bone-meal powder
Brewers' yeast
Desiccated liver
Eggs
High-protein powder
Gelatin
Lecithin granules
Rose-hip powder

Suggested Readings

BOOKS AND PAMPHLETS

Agricultural Handbook #8 (Composition of Foods). Washington: U.S. Department of Agriculture.

Airola, Paavo. *Sex and Nutrition*. New York: Award Books, 1970.

Bailey, Herbert. *Vitamin Pioneers*. Emmaus, Pa.: Rodale Press, 1968.

—————. *Your Key to a Healthy Heart: The Suppressed Record of Vitamin E*. Philadelphia: Chilton Book Company, 1964.

Bicknell and Prescott. *The Vitamins in Medicine*. Milwaukee: Lee Foundation for Nutritional Research.

Bieler, Henry G. *Food Is Your Best Medicine*. New York: Random House, 1965.

Brady, William. *Secrets of Positive Health*. New York: Prentice-Hall, 1961.

Cantor, Alfred J. *Doctor Cantor's Longevity Diet: How to Slow Down Aging and Prolong Youth and Vigor*. New York, Prentice-Hall, 1967.

Cheraskin, E., and Ringdorf, W. M., Jr. *New Hope for Incurable Diseases*. Jericho, N.Y.: Exposition Press, 1971.

Davis, Adelle. *Let's Cook It Right*. Rev. ed. New York: Harcourt Brace Jovanovich, 1962.

—————. *Let's Eat Right to Keep Fit*. Rev. ed. New York: Harcourt Brace Jovanovich, 1970.

181

————. *Let's Get Well.* New York: Harcourt Brace Jovanovich, 1965.

————. *Let's Have Healthy Children.* New and exp. ed. New York: Harcourt Brace Jovanovich, 1972.

Ellis, John M. *The Doctor Who Looked at Hands.* New York: Arc Books, 1970.

Funk, Casimir. *Vitamines.* 1922.

Hoffer, Abram, and Osmond, Humphry. *How to Live with Schizophrenia.* New Hyde Park, N.Y.: University Books, 1966.

Hunter, Beatrice Turm. *Beatrice Turm Hunter's Whole-Grain Baking Sampler.* New Canaan, Conn.: Keats Publishing, 1972.

————. *Consumer, Beware.* New York. Simon & Schuster, 1971.

————. *Fact-Book on Additives.* New Canaan, Conn.: Keats Publishing, 1972.

————. *Gardening Without Poison.* 2nd ed. Boston: Houghton-Mifflin Company, 1972.

————. *Natural Foods Cookbook.* New York: Simon & Schuster, 1972.

————. *The Natural Foods Primer.* New York: Simon & Schuster, 1972.

Jarvis, D. C. *Arthritis and Folk Medicine.* New York: Holt, Rinehart and Winston, 1960.

————. *Folk Medicine: A Vermont Doctor's Guide to Good Health.* New York: Holt, Rinehart and Winston, 1958.

Klenner, Fred R., and Bartz, Frederick. *The Key to Good Health, Vitamin C: Don't Lose This Key.* Chicago: Graphic Arts Research Foundation, 1969.

Pauling, Linus. *Vitamin C and the Common Cold.* 5th ed. San Francisco: W. H. Freeman and Company, 1970.

Roberts, Sam E. *Ear, Nose and Throat Dysfunctions.* Springfield, Ill.: Charles C. Thomas, 1957.

————. *Exhaustion: Causes and Treatment.* Emmaus, Pa.: Rodale Press, 1967.

Sherman, Henry C. *Calcium and Phosphorus in Foods and Nutrition.* New York: Columbia University Press, 1947.

————. *Chemistry of Food and Nutrition.* 8th ed. 1946. New York: The Macmillan Company, 1952.

————. *Food and Health.* New ed. New York: The Macmillan Company, 1946.

————. *Foods: Their Value and Management.* 1946.

————. *The Nutritional Improvement of Life.* 1950.

————, and Lanford, C. S. *Essentials of Nutrition.* 3rd ed. New York. The Macmillan Company, 1951.

————, and Smith, S. L. *The Vitamins.* Rev. ed. 1931.

Shute, E. V. *Alpha-Tocopherol (Vitamin E) in Cardiovascular Disease.* Old Greenwich, Conn.: Devin-Adair, 1959.

Williams, Roger J. *Nutrition Against Disease.* New York: Pitman, 1971.

Wood, H. Curtis. *Calories, Vitamins, and Common Sense.* New York: Belmont Books.

Vine, Lesley. *Ecological Eating.* New York: Tower Books.

PERIODICALS

Let's Live. Oxford Industries, 444 North Larchmont Boulevard, Los Angeles, Calif. 90004.

Natural Foods and Farming. Natural Foods Associates, P.O. Box 210, Atlanta, Texas, 75551.

Organic Gardening. Rodale Press, Emmaus, Pa.

Prevention. Rodale Press, Emmaus, Pa.

INDEX OF RECIPES